To Jim,

"Expect the Best"

Blessings,

Stoff

"The content is superb, writing is superb, and there is a mixture of a story and great information . . . I suggest you read it!"

—Art Bauer
CEO of Media Learning International

"The acorn does not fall far from the 'Batten Tree'! I think this book is going to do exceptionally well."

—Lance Farrell
CEO of Farrell's Extreme Body Shaping

"You have in your hands a collage of the best practices in sales, service, leadership, and a host of other lessons, all told in a highly readable fashion. Coupled with a series of self-assessments, you possess a vast array of proven tips and techniques. You are already well on your way to the artistry of your own excellence."

—Edward E. Scannell, CMP, CSP
Co-author of *Games Trainers Play* series

"A modern guide founded on time-tested principles. Steve Havemann hits the mark in expounding upon the nuggets of wisdom originated by Joe Batten. Whether you are a seasoned sales professional or starting out in a new sales role, take the story of Bryce Norman slowly and reflect on the insight that is masterfully woven into the mentor-mentee storyline."

—Matthew Michalak
Sales Professional

The Excellent Persuader

The Excellent Persuader

By
Steve Havemann
And Joe D. Batten

RESOURCE *Publications* • Eugene, Oregon

THE EXCELLENT PERSUADER

Resource Publications
An Imprint of Wipf and Stock Publishers
199 W. 8th Ave., Suite 3
Eugene, OR 97401

www.wipfandstock.com

ISBN 13: 978-1-62564-066-6

Manufactured in the U.S.A.

Grandpa, you were the kindest, strongest, and wisest man I've ever known. Thank you for teaching me:

- To always hoe to the end of the row.
- To operate with dignity and decorum.
- That a promise made is a debt unpaid.
- That each individual on this planet is a bundle of present and potential strengths.
- That there are no greater values in life than honesty, integrity, accountability, and respect.
- To love unconditionally.
- That good is derived from God.
- To prioritize life and professional goals constantly.
- That you become what you think.
- To dare to dream, and put muscle behind your dreams.
- To expect the best from others.
- That attitude is everything!
- To "Be All That You Can Be."
- That "goodfellowship" is a way of life

With more respect, love, gratitude, and great memories than words can ever describe.

Your good buddy,

Steven

"We are all salespeople every day of our lives, selling our ideas and enthusiasm to those with whom we come in contact!"

—CHARLES SCHWAB

Contents

Foreword

JOE BATTEN WAS ONE of my closest friends in the author/speaker/consultant profession. We met for the first time shortly after the publication of Joe's landmark book, *Tough-Minded Management,* and my book, *Management by Objectives and Results.* We remained close friends for more than 35 years. I had the privilege of speaking and singing at his memorial service a few years ago. Consequently, I was excited when his grandson, Steve Havemann, contacted me several months ago to tell me that he planned to complete a book that he and Joe had started writing shortly before his untimely death and would appreciate my assistance. I jumped at the opportunity.

The Excellent Persuader has captured the story-telling style of Joe Batten while bringing profound insights into the transformation of a struggling salesman into a true sales professional in today's society. It incorporates the role of a mentor, Mr. Jackson, (a favorite Batten technique) as a guide to keeping the "human factor" in the sales process.

If you remember Joe Batten, you will revel in this new contribution to the world of business writing. If you are not familiar with him, you are in for a treat as you experience the Batten/Havemann style of bringing common-sense learning as applied to today's business challenges.

George Morrisey
Author of 19 books including
Management by Objectives and Results and *Morrisey on Planning* three-book series

Introduction

ACCORDING TO THE U.S. Bureau of Labor Statistics, one in nine Americans works in sales, meaning that each day more than fifteen million people earn their keep by persuading someone else to make a purchase.

The Excellent Persuader is a sales and management development book that follows the life, trials, and tribulations of a struggling salesman, Bryce Norman. Through his connection with a veteran sales, management, training, and human resource development guru, Bryce begins to learn what it means to become a true sales "Artist." Throughout his journey of personal growth, he learns how to develop himself and develop others, while drastically altering the trajectory of his professional and personal life.

The following text has the unique ability to reach organizational leaders at every level. Leaders and sales professionals whether entry-level, veteran, or manager will be guided through the *art* of how to become an "Excellent Persuader" by utilizing the techniques and specific strategies outlined in this resource. Through the use of sales, human resource development, management and leadership techniques, *The Excellent Persuader* provides the tools in a reader-friendly manner to alter the paradigm through which the struggling, average, above-average, or over-eager sales professionals approach their profession. Concerns voiced by sales leaders are addressed throughout, as well as specific techniques to educate, re-frame, or re-invent individuals' approaches to sales.

1

The Problem

Bryce Norman is having trouble with his job of selling. His boss is clamping down on him, his customers are beginning to turn away, and he is getting scared, walking on eggshells at work and just trying to survive every day. His sales are obviously dropping, and there's more. He is considering making a career switch if things don't turn around. The economy has been tough, and expenses are piling up at home. Braces, car repair, tutoring, and athletic fees are all adding up. Bryce's wife Samantha is just about ready to give up and get a second job, and tensions are high. Bryce doesn't know what he is going to do to better his situation, but he knows that something must change!

The face peering back from the mirror at young Bryce Norman looked grim and set. It seemed to leer at him. "How are you going to pay for Emme's braces? For Eric's new shoes? The car needs new tires and the house needs new windows. Maybe it is time to give up on your dreams and switch jobs. Maybe you should work somewhere that you can just put in your time." He couldn't help but think, "Bryce Norman, you're a failure!"

"What if's" had begun to encompass Bryce's daily and hourly thoughts. "What if I can't pay the bills?" "What if we can't cover the dental work that Emme needs?" "What if the car finally breaks down?" These thoughts spun in Bryce's head as he fastened a Timex watch around his wrist. They continued, "What if the economy doesn't get better? Should I take a second job?"

With that, Bryce kissed Samantha goodbye and headed for work, taking only a moment to breathe in the spring air before climbing in for the commute.

2

Meet Mr. Jackson

IN THE MEANTIME, CLAYTON Sanchez was discouraged. CEO of the Pinnacle Company, he had been in the job seven years, and a lot of good things had happened. However, he wasn't feeling well; something was eating at him from the inside out. Clayton's piercing gaze focused on the quarterly sales data in front of him. The staff simply weren't producing at the level he felt was possible. Leaning back in his chair, Clayton thought back to his mentor and former boss, Mr. Jackson. He was widely considered the "sales training dean of America." It was time, Clayton decided, to call his old boss and ask for some guidance. Reluctantly, he picked up his phone, scrolled through his contacts, and dialed.

Mr. Jackson asked Clayton to clear his calendar for the afternoon on the following Friday, and he would come by at 1:00 sharp. It had been seven years since Clayton had seen Mr. Jackson, he wondered, "Does he still have it? Can he help me? Is he still at the cutting edge of business?"

Six days later, at 12:50, Clayton got a call notifying him Mr. Jackson had arrived. Waiting on the other side of the door was Mr. Jackson, who incredibly, (with the exception of more grey hair) looked no older than he had years ago. His eyes still had an attentive, almost piercing dynamic to them. He wore a navy blue pin stripe suit that was clearly fresh from the cleaners accompanied with a subtle red tie. He stood confidently, and seemed to stand taller and straighter than even Clayton remembered.

The two warmly greeted each other and adjourned to Clayton's office.

Confident that the Pinnacle Corporation has the best products in the market, Clayton began to outline the struggles of the sales division.

"I'm really proud of a lot of the things we've done here. Our products are amongst the best in the industry. Our facilities and financial stability are outstanding. I'm proud of just about everything in the company, except our sales division; they simply aren't producing."

3

The Mentor Responds

<small>MOMENTS PASSED, AND THEN</small> Mr. Jackson asked:

"Clayton, will you tell me more about the sales division? Who works there? What kinds of people are in it? What kind of training do they receive? What kind of sales kits, promotional materials, and literature do you have? What kind of technology training do you provide? What kind of criteria do you use when you promote a person?"

Clayton leaned forward eagerly and his voice crackled with vitality.

"We hire people who seem to want to drive to the top. I want people who can really run an operation and tell people what's good for them, and tell them why they should buy our products. They are pushers, drivers, with the ability to really pitch. That's what we hire, and we've done a great job teaching them to do this."

"Are they all like this?" Mr. Jackson *asked*.

"No," Clayton said, "We're particularly disappointed in one person, Bryce Norman. He just can't seem to get with it and sell the way we tell our people to. He's got great academic credentials, appears to possess the soft skills to succeed, knows how to dress, has a resonant voice, seems pretty confident, and really *looks* like a pro, but he can't seem to cut it here."

"How would you feel about Bryce and me meeting to talk things over next Tuesday?" asked Mr. Jackson.

Clayton looked please and said, "I'll arrange for him to meet you here that morning."

4

Bryce's Quandary

AFTER BRYCE'S SENIOR MANAGER told him to clear his schedule for the following Wednesday, his mind began to spiral. "Wonder why they want me to meet with this Mr. Jackson guy? Am I going to get fired, chewed out? What? Why doesn't he just retire and go play golf?" Bryce squirmed all weekend, dreading his perceived impending doom. He had, after all, decided he wanted to excel in sales, and he used to believe he had the skill set to advance rapidly.

As Tuesday inched by, Bryce stressed more and more. He couldn't lose his job; he had too much at stake. Sure things weren't going well right now, but he did believe they could get better. The next morning Bryce strode purposefully down the hall toward what, he imagined, could be impending doom.

As Bryce approached the door, Mr. Jackson stood up and said cordially, "How are you Bryce? Will you have a seat?"

Bryce cautiously sat down, wondering to himself when he'd start to "get the word." He asked Mr. Jackson a little suddenly, "Are you going to tell me what to do, how to the hit the mark, how to drive, how to project enthusiasm?"

Mr. Jackson grinned, "I'm not going to tell you anything Bryce. Rather, I'd like to learn a lot about you, who you really are."

"But, I thought . . ."

"Yes, I imagine what you thought; the question is, will you *let* me get to know you and your work?"

"Well, sure, but I guess I'm a little surprised because nobody in management has been *asking* me anything. They do a lot of *telling* here."

Mr. Jackson began to ask Bryce question after question. He wanted to know more about Bryce's dreams, his hopes, his likes, his dislikes, his joys and frustrations, what he read, how he felt about his family and friends.

The hours evaporated and Bryce felt a kind of therapeutic effect as he poured out thoughts, feelings, and goals. Mr. Jackson was carefully building on strengths that he saw in Bryce, not dwelling on perceived weaknesses.

Mr. Jackson glanced at his watch, "Can you meet with me again tomorrow Bryce? Say 8:30? I'm only in town for a couple of days this week."

"Let me rearrange my schedule" Bryce responded, "I'm already looking forward to it. I'll bring the coffee."

"Oh, one thing," said Mr. Jackson, "will you sit down with your wife this evening and, between the two of you, write down every strength you can brainstorm about Bryce Norman?"

Bryce smiled, "You know, I'm not sure I could have thought of any if we hadn't talked this morning, but, yeah, I'll write down every strength that I can think of."

5

A New Beginning

THAT NIGHT BRYCE AND Samantha had a long talk. Mr. Jackson had started all sorts of internal dialog for Bryce. He was now thinking about things like: purpose, direction, goals, and vitality.

As he and his wife shared thoughts about each other's strengths, and as Bryce began to hesitantly list his strengths, he felt the beginning of the kind of enthusiasm he had not felt for years. It was a feeling of anticipation in his mind, body, and spirit.

After listing over 25 strengths, he finally came to a stopping point. He knew there were more, and his goal was to reach 100, but it was now 10:30 and his brain was spinning. He decided, "I think I'll write out all those expectations Mr. Jackson mentioned."

Then, even though his wife and kids had gone to bed, Bryce proceeded to think and write. A little after midnight, he had finished three separate lists of expectations. They were:

1. What he expected from other people in his life.

2. What he expected from God

3. What he expected from himself.

Feeling tired, but good, Bryce crawled into bed. Somehow, things seemed to be coming together.

He slept.

The next day, Bryce and Mr. Jackson reviewed his strengths and expectations, and then paused for a cup of coffee.

"Okay, Bryce, we're ready to talk about and think about your possibilities as a total person, but particularly as a salesman. How do you answer when someone asks you what you do for a living?

"I say, I sell for a living. In fact, Mr. Sanchez describes our sales team as the most driven group of sales professionals in the country. Somehow, though, I'm beginning to think that's kind of a poor way to describe selling for a living."

"Selling for a living, is that really all you see yourself doing?"

"Well, I know it takes a lot of *skill* to make a good living in this game. I guess I'd like to, at least, be thought of as practicing a skill."

Mr. Jackson grew very earnest. "Bryce, as you know, I've trained and developed literally thousands of sales people, and I've yet to see a truly great one who sees himself as a sales-craftsman or product pusher."

"The great ones know that they are more than Pros (and there aren't nearly enough Pros); they are *Artists*!"

Bryce furrowed his brow. "A sales artist? I see art as sculptures, paintings, maybe even negotiation. And they have to be good at what they do."

"Bingo," said Mr. Jackson, "all of these individuals are artists because they are the best at what they do, not because they create things with paint."

"You are an artist that is dedicated to helping your clients not only reach, but exceed their goals. Your goal is not to sell them products, but rather provide a service to your clients, and when you ask to be compensated for your work, they will not be surprised. A *real* artist, no matter what he or she does, is committed to certain *principles*, and these, Bryce, are *crucial* to a life of richness, achievement, and fulfillment. I hope you'll really think about them. "

"Well," Bryce said, "I'd really like to know what they are. I'm still fairly young and I'd like to make my life as productive as possible.'"

Mr. Jackson pursed his lips and began to tick these principles off slowly:

1. *Service*-At the heart of all great *pro*fessions such as medicine, the law, human resource development, ministry, education, etc., is a pledge of service. When we provide truly superior service in every dimension of our job and our life, we build richness — financially, socially, spiritually, and emotionally. We find ourselves by losing ourselves in service to others.

2. *Education*-An open, growing quality of mind, fueled by a sense of wonder and curiosity is the hallmark of the truly educated person. The best specialist is one who is constantly studying and learning many things. In sales, it is important to study human behavior, negotiation and how to truly listen to the customer.

3. *Attitude*-The winning attitude is always one which is basically fueled by faith, hope, wonder, love, and gratitude. These, in turn, fuel a commitment to excellent product knowledge, customer-caring, and the

confidence to close sales. In short, they fuel and feed a commitment to that beautiful four-letter word known as work.

4. *Discipline*-This means "training which builds, molds and strengthens." Out of discipline flow the 3-D's of successful selling. They are *dedication, determination, and desire*."

Bryce broke in, "Is integrity a part of this?"

"Yes," said Mr. Jackson, "but integrity is not a basic quality, it is a *product* of these four."

Bryce followed-up, "I feel like I'm ready to get out there and make an impact. What else can I do?"

"We haven't really talked yet about what I call 'The Continuum of Actualization,' but that can wait. We'll be discussing elements of it after you've gone out and set some appointments."

"Will I be meeting with you frequently?" inquired Bryce.

"Only until you've discovered how it feels to experience selling and living as an art," replied Mr. Jackson.

"So what can I do next?" Bryce continued.

"What do you think?" Mr. Jackson replied.

"Well, I should probably start making some calls and setting appointments," Bryce said earnestly.

Mr. Jackson smiled and said, "Exactly! Really try to visualize every selling situation as an important date. Remember when you first began dating your wife? I'll bet you prepared for every date by looking, feeling, and sounding just as interesting and caring as you could. Then, I'll bet you felt a little rush of healthy adrenaline, and you hoped she'd be happy about the date; right?"

"True," Bryce said, "And I also did some thinking about the right timing, place, and atmosphere."

"Do you see what I'm getting at Bryce? Can we get together a week from today?"

"Deal, thank you!" beamed Bryce. "In the meantime, I'm going to make some appointments and give them my best shot."

"Okay, Bryce, give them your best shot, and we'll review what happened next week. Oh, by the way, my definition of excellence is to give a thing your best shot and know it."

6

What Happened

WALKING FROM THE PARKING lot at Seven Resources, Bryce mentally rehearsed his presentation to Mike Norris, Purchasing Agent.

He discovered his mind was in more turmoil than he had expected. What had Mr. Jackson said? What had changed?

Bryce paused on the sidewalk for a minute and thought back to Mr. Jackson's words, "Determine what you expect from life. Begin to visualize yourself as a walking bundle of present and potential strengths. Decide whether you'll settle for just selling for a living or whether you want to be a craftsman, a semi-pro, a pro, or an *Artist* at persuasion. Feel *great* about yourself and what you're becoming."

Bryce could see Mr. Jackson saying, "Fundamental principles in today's life and work style of the *Pro* and *Artist* include service, education, attitude, and discipline. Plan and prepare like you would for a date when you go to meet with the customer. Feel a little rush of healthy adrenaline (also known as nerves) as you walk in."

As he walked down the hall to Mike Norris' office, the feeling of turmoil was still there. Bryce had been pretty thoroughly trained in the methods of Clayton Sanchez to push, drive, dominate the relationship; to pitch his products and focus on the money he'd get. Bryce realized, even as he shook hands with Mr. Norris, that he wasn't yet using Mr. Jackson's approach, "Ask, listen and hear to determine wants, needs, and possibilities."

Bryce was beginning to comprehend the new approach, but he didn't really know how to implement it yet.

He smiled cordially, gave Mr. Norris a warm, firm handshake and began his presentation. Here are the highlights:

"Mike, I want to tell you about our products. They are the best in the industry . . ."

"According to our surveys, everybody in your industry needs these products and I'm going to see that you get the best."

"You won't regret this decision . . .

"I shouldn't be telling you this, but . . .

"This way you won't have to make any changes for years . . .

"I'm telling you, if I were in your shoes I would . . ."

As Bryce continued to dominate, tell, and 'present,' he became aware that Mike Norris just wasn't warming up. In fact, he seemed to be growing rather remote and cold. Every time he glanced at his phone, Bryce increased his tempo and volume. Finally, with a fixed smile, Mike Norris got to his feet and said in an even voice, "Mr. Norman, I appreciate the time you've taken and I'm sure Pinnacle has good products, but right now we're not going to make a decision on this. Maybe some other time."

Bryce walked out feeling dejected. "I don't get it. I went in there and gave it my best shot, but just couldn't close. Well, I've got two more appointments today; maybe I'm not coming on strong enough . . ."

Every call seemed to somehow backfire. The next afternoon he called Mr. Jackson and confirmed their appointment.

Mr. Jackson asked Bryce to be prepared to share with him exactly what had happened at his meetings, so Bryce prepared diligently to do this.

They were to meet Thursday morning, but in the meantime, Bryce had several more appointments with very little success. He looked a little down and dispirited.

Before Thursday, Mr. Jackson called his friend, Mike Norris, and had a candid and cordial chat about the kind of salespeople he preferred, what he wanted, what he needed, and what he saw as the "ideal" sales/ buying conversation. Further research had him ready for Bryce.

Bryce arrived five minutes early for his appointment with Mr. Jackson. He was welcomed in and offered a chair across from Mr. Jackson.

"Good Morning Bryce," Mr. Jackson exuded, "so how did your appointment with Mike Norris go? How do you feel about the whole thing?" he asked.

Bryce began to reconstruct his conversation with Mike Norris, and Mr. Jackson listened, jotted notes, and took a sip of coffee.

After a minute he said, "You know, Bryce, you're making the effort to learn, you're dressing more sharply, and you're maintaining a positive, open attitude. As such, you're more than a peddler right now, but we've got to work on giving you the kind of real tools to become at Pro, then we'll see what you want to shoot for beyond that, but it takes time. Remember, Bryce, the most valuable assets in business today are positive, productive relationships."

The whiteboard filled several times as they talked, thought, and wrote. Bryce was becoming excited. Here were the *tools* he had yearned for:

- "When you ask, you find out more and you show you care."

- "When you listen, the customer feels good about things."

- "When you hear, you move into an ideal position to close, because you are identifying the wants, needs, and possibilities of the customer!"

- "When you tell, you diminish the dignity of your customer."

- "It is not enough to determine their *wants* and *needs*, help them think through and realize possibilities for greater efficiency, cost effectiveness, and innovation."

- "The amateur salesperson does 90% of the talking and 10% of the listening."

- "The Pro does 90% of the listening and 10% of the talking."

- "The amateur is a cynic. The Pro has a sense of wonder and high expectations."

- "The amateur blames the customer when they don't buy. The Pro knows that whenever you point a finger there are three pointing back at you—and that's about the right proportion or ratio."

- "The amateur manipulates-the Pro fulfills."

- "The amateur thinks people want to feel important. The Pro knows they *need* to feel *significant*."

- "When we push, we become compressed, repressed and depressed . . . and we get worn down."

- "When we stay open, flexible, and grateful, we are constantly renewed and we grow, change and move ahead."

- "The power of a *question* is infinitely greater than that of a declarative or directive statement."

- "The 20% who go back after five rejections accomplish 80% of the sales."

- "You become rich in your wallet when you become rich in your mind."

- "Amateurs are dissatisfied-they park beside yesterday's failures and become diminished."

- "Pros are unsatisfied—they consistently strive to excel in all things and can usually learn something from every situation."

- "Pros stay curious; they develop a real thirst for personal growth, knowledge, and mentally challenging situations."

- "Amateurs—peddlers, have either forgotten how to dream or are afraid to."

- "Pros let their dreams nourish and fuel all of their goals and actions."

- "Amateurs are pinched, tight and defensive."

- "Pros enjoy letting themselves 'out' and letting other people 'in.'"

- "Amateurs want to be successful; Pros decide to be successful."

- "The amateur thinks—"When you've seen one, you've seen them all." The Pro believes there is something unique, significant, and possibly splendid in every person and every tour of the customer's premises."

- "The Pro relishes giving genuine compliments and praise-and *does* so often."

- "The Pro knows and constantly demonstrates that the more you give, the more you get."

- "The Pro genuinely believes that when you ask people to buy your product or service you are literally doing a good thing *for* them."

- "The amateur has quit growing, learning and expanding. The Pro constantly cultivates a flexible, open, growing, changing, and questing mind."

- "The Tough-Minded Pro is secure enough to often say, 'I've got a problem and I need your help.'"

- "The amateur becomes stiffened and stultified by fear. The Pro recognizes the positivism and potential of fear."

- "The Pro is committed to relationships. He wants to be very sure that the customer will look forward to seeing him/her come back again."

"Now, that was a lot of information" said Mr. Jackson, "but stay with me for a little longer." "The following six key elements combine to allow us to use what the acronym spells and enable us to learn how to recognize our possibilities. They are:

"G—Goals, visions and dreams

"R—Realistic assessment of strengths

"O—Openness and emotional vulnerability

"W—Wonder (a sense of)

"T—Tough-Minded expectations

"H—Hope

"Dare to let your mind go forth and dare to dream. What would you optimally like to be and do? Only accept your optimum dream. Confront your possibilities and think through and write down (in five sentences or less) the overall stretching goal that will enrich, stretch, and condition all that you think, say, do, and are. Learn to love the word *"goal."* Display it in a visible place that is a constant reminder. Share it, talk about it, and live it. That's the "G."

"*Realistic assessment of strengths* means just that. We are all walking bundles of strengths and possibilities. Our "weaknesses" are only missing, underdeveloped, or undiscovered strengths. This knowledge alone can dramatically affect your life and everything you become. We need to build a strength-centered culture, which is a true motivational climate. Our strengths are our tools. Our strengths are who we are! Focusing on "weaknesses" can be a sure route to de-motivation, failure and emotional oblivion.

"*Openness and vulnerability.* Each of the six G.R.O.W.T.H. elements progress sequentially. As we think through and clarify our macro goals, vision, and dreams, and as we launch an all-out program to discover our present and potential strengths, we then become capable of interacting with others with our emotional and mental guards down. We let others in and let ourselves out. We learn to diffuse, defuse, and dissolve our defenses.

"Vulnerability in this context does not mean physical vulnerability. But, when we open our minds, hearts and souls and let challenges, difficulties, and triumphs in, we must constantly search for, and find, new strengths. It's a recipe for never-ending growth and motivation.

"The sense of *Wonder* is developed through a positive outlook on life. It is a full-time, lifelong quest that persists in seeking out the wonder, the beauty-enhancing qualities of people, events, and things. A study of the greatest motivators and leaders of history (Master Motivators) will reveal conclusively that they never ceased to look for the beauty, possibilities, and strengths in all things.

"*Tough-Minded expectations* are the standards we hold ourselves to on our own personal journey towards our possibilities. It is imperative to set high personal standards and strive to exceed them if we are to successfully elicit and evoke the best from others. Tough-Mindedness is a series of paradigm shifts. Being *Tough-Minded* does not mean being hard, it means being resilient and open. You see, the *Tough-Minded* individual is like a piece of leather. When leather is hit by a sledge hammer, it merely dents, and eventually regains its previous shape. The hard—minded individual is like a piece of granite. When granite is hit with a significant blow, it simply shatters into hundreds of unrecognizable pieces." Mr. Jackson drew the following thoughts on the Smart Board:

Paradigm Shifts for the Tough-Minded Individual

From:	To:
Hard-mindedness	Tough-Mindedness
Activity centered	Results centered
Negative	Positive and enthusiastic
Fragile	Durable
Rigid	Flexible
Grim	Cheerful
Arrogant	Poised, yet warm
Go-getter	Go-giver
Expects the worst	Expects the best
Static	Confident of future
Fearful	Strong and resilient
Abrasive, blunt	Candid
Dwells on weakness	Building on strengths
Pushes, drives	Leads

Low expectations of self and others	High expectations of self and others

"You see, perhaps the finest gift you can give another person is the gift of an excellent and stretching expectation based on a never-ending search for present and potential strengths. When you study the strengths of others, you are able to see their possibilities, and the more you study their strengths, the better you are qualified to temper your expectations with reality and reason.

"Please reflect on this again and again. It is a gigantic step toward becoming a true artist. If you don't expect the best from yourself and others, what is the alternative?

"The final component of the G.R.O.W.T.H. sequence is *Hope*. It is not only crucial, it is absolutely essential to all positive motivation. Every successful sale, every successful personal transaction, all successful teaching experiences, will only occur if the recipient has sufficient hope concerning the outcome."

"Hold it," Bryce Laughed, "I just don't know if I can absorb any more, I've got to get out and begin to work on these things."

With twinkling eyes Mr. Jackson nodded, "Right, but first let's make sure we've got this whole value system and tool kit in place. We've been recording all of this, and I'd recommend that you listen to this conversation until you know it backwards and forwards."

"Then, I'd also recommend that you transcribe it. The visual image of the printed word strengthens additional dimensions of your mind, and helps insure that your actual behavior, your way of doing things, changes."

"Let's move on then," Bryce exclaimed, "this is what I've been waiting for!"

Mr. Jackson launched back into the conversation without missing a beat.

- "You will eventually get what you expect; we all *become* what we expect."

- "Stock and fill your subconscious mind with power thoughts and positive expectations. Then, relax and let them go to work."

- "The Pro will always leave the customer believing more in him or herself."

- "The Tough-Minded, vulnerable Pro is secure enough to ask for help."

- "The amateur becomes stiffened and stultified by fear. The Pro recognizes the positivism and potential of fear."

- "The Pro sells one thing at a time."

- "The Pro is committed to building relationships and social capital. He/she wants to be very sure that the customer will look forward to seeing him/her come back again."

- "The true Pro gets up in front of the group and he/she probably has even more tension than the amateur, but this tension is flowing out from him/her and reaching out and enveloping, affecting and energizing the audience."

Bryce interjected, "These are tremendous things for the Pro to do, but can you share some more things about the kind of person he is or can become?"

"With pleasure," Mr. Jackson grinned.

"All personal growth is made through the willingness to accept change. Are you willing to accept change, Bryce?"

Bryce responded enthusiastically, "I'm ready!"

"All great leaders challenge themselves and others to accomplish great things. So here are my challenges for you Bryce. Begin with one of them, then add a new one each week. Soon they will become habits, and that is when true personal growth occurs."

1. "Do you dare to compete only with yourself? Only the amateur competes with others."

2. "Dare to judge yourself by results, not activity. Lots of calls and lots of notions do no good unless you close."

3. "Dare to root cynicism and sarcasm totally out of your vocabulary. Pros are too busy building on strengths to dwell on negatives and perceived weaknesses."

4. "Dare to become excited by the possibilities of your positive candor (social capital)."

5. "Dare to apologize when you know you have done your best, but never apologize for something before you give it your best shot."

6. "Dare to be accountable for your actions."

7. "Dare to let enthusiasm infuse your every action, your voice, your face, your body language, your every movement."

8. "Dare to radiate love. Hate is for the gutless and confused."

9. "Dare to make a real study of the profit motive and its scriptural underpinning."

10. "Dare to become and stay emotionally open. Closed off people become rigid, static, non-productive, and unhealthy. It is a shortcut towards physical, mental, and spiritual deterioration."

11. "Dare to doubt your doubts!"

12. "Dare to believe that what you are thunders so loud they'll want to hear what you say."

Mr. Jackson paused, glanced around the room and looked at the clock. "Okay Bryce, you've certainly got a lot to process, and enough challenges to keep you busy. Later on, after you've become the kind of Pro I know you can be we'll zero in on what it takes to function at the pinnacle of sales, or any other professions, the level of *art*."

7

The New Style is Attempted

BRYCE SPENT MOST OF Friday planning his appointments for the following week. Both he and Mr. Jackson were focusing in on a Batten, Batten, Hudson, and Swab training film entitled, "Manage Your Time to Build Your Territory," and he had become intrigued with the concept of S.M.A.R.T. planning. It shaped up like this:

> *Schedule your time*
>
> *Make time*
>
> *Allow time*
>
> *Ration time*
>
> *Take time*

Each step held some interesting possibilities:

Schedule your time—set up a schedule with two columns, one with the heading *"Must Do"* and the other column heading entitled *"Want to Do."* Rank your musts in order of priority, and make sure they are all attended to before you devote any time to your wants. This sounds amazingly simple, but it requires:

a. Thought

b. Self-discipline

c. Determination

d. Dedication

Make time—organize and write down your key thoughts before each sales call. List possible objections. After each call jot down facts, ideas, and feelings which will make your next call more profitable.

Allow time—stay flexible. Develop an alternate plan. If things go wrong, be prepared with another alternative.

Ration time—ration time so that most of it goes to the potentially most profitable customers. Divide your customers in three groups, A, B, and C with your best customers and prospects in group A, average customers and prospects in group B, and the less profitable accounts in group C. Ration most of your time to the A group. Use the telephone to maintain contact with the B and C groups so that you know when and if a personal call is justified.

Take time—the idea isn't to make *calls*, but to foster new relationships and make *sales*. Take the extra hour in the morning or the evening. Take the time for the follow up or phone call to ensure customer satisfaction, and don't underestimate the power of a thank you note.

After discussing this approach, Mr. Jackson shared these thoughts with Bryce:

1. Show me how you use your "spare" time and I will show you what and where you will be ten years from now.

2. No person is paid for their time. They are paid for the use they make of it.

3. The use of one's time determines the space one acquires in this world.

4. You will find time for all your needs if you have yourself properly organized.

5. Develop a weekly list of major "musts" and "wants." Rank them in priority order and do all the musts before pursuing the wants.

6. Develop a daily list of "musts" and "wants." Rank them in priority order and do all the musts before pursuing the wants.

These efforts result in Excellent Management of Time 'n' Territory, which adds up to TNT!

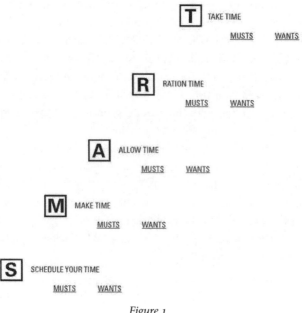

Figure 1

On Monday, Bryce was up early, went for a jog, ate a good breakfast, prepared for the day, and headed to work feeling better than he could remember!

His first appointment was with Greg Walker, Executive Vice President of Hearthstone Solutions. Mr. Walker was a very busy man and accustomed to dealing with specifics. When Bryce began his Asking-Listening-Hearing approach, he smiled and said casually, "Mr. Walker, will you tell me about Hearthstone? I want to know all about it."

Mr. Walker fixed him with a piercing glance and said, "Why?"

Caught off guard, Bryce stammered, "Well, I want to ask, listen, and hear to determine your wants, needs, and possibilities."

Mr. Walker cynically lifted an eyebrow and again said, "Why?"

Bryce told him, somewhat lamely, that he was just "interested" in Hearthstone and that's why. . .well. . .why. . .

Greg Walker was, after all, a kind man, and he said, "Bryce, I like you. You're a smart enough guy, but you should get your act together and make very sure you don't waste people's time. Our time is just about up now, but I'd be glad to arrange some time in, let's say, about thirty days."

Mr. Walker's remarks left a deep impression on Bryce. He resolved to be fully prepared the next time.

Bryce walked out, and before his next call, jotted down a few insights that were dawning on him.

1. I'm beginning to understand the qualities of a Pro.

2. I'm beginning to schedule myself and my time effectively.

3. I must organize my presentation.

4. I must develop insights into the uniqueness of each customer.

The rest of the week was a steady learning process. New insights kept coming to him, and he was experimenting with many of the ideas he'd gotten from Mr. Jackson. He was determined to "get his act together."

On Saturday he assembled his notes, began to really synthesize and reflect upon his learning, which resulted in a four-step "presentation procedure."

Bryce wrote:

My Presentation Procedure

1. Begin with a powerful, caring, informed question! This will get immediate, favorable attention. The purpose of these questions is to grab your audience's favorable attention, energy and curiosity with a stimulating and challenging question or statement.

    For Example:

    a. How much profit would you like to make?

    b. Do you know where your major costs are?

    c. What would you most like—ideally—to have happen in this job/company?

2. Relate to my audience! Seek to discover what may be unique about my customer. There is always at least one unique want, need, problem, or possibility. You can find it if you *care* enough. Quickly find your prospect's real interests and then focus your selling efforts on satisfying that interest. Don't forget to do your research ahead of time!

3. Get my audience "into the act" through participation and involvement. Remember, real client participation is necessary to obtain commitment and conviction to the agreement you are seeking. Many salespeople have talked their way out of a sale instead of into one. Stimulate prospects' active participation. Get them to talk and discuss, get agreement from them as you go

along. Get participation in your demonstration.

4. Close on cue! Watch carefully to know when you need to close. A word of *caution*: sometimes the customer is ready to buy before all possibilities for more and larger sales have been explored. Don't procrastinate, but don't rush! Be confident in the fact that you have: *asked, listened and heard* your client in order to determine *wants, needs, and possibilities*.

As Bryce reflected upon these procedures, he decided to add some thought starters:

My Thought Starters

1. What is the most powerful, a statement or a question? Mr. Jackson told me a question, if it is imaginative enough, always is. I'll test this until I'm sure.

2. How can I put my customer totally at ease? I'm determined to find some significant strengths in every person I call on. I'll do it!

Mr. Jackson had stressed that planning, organizing, and acting should be done effectively, and then efficiently. That is, the *pro* makes sure he/she is doing the *right thing* rather than just *doing things right*.

Bryce decided to go the extra mile to ensure that his presentation improved continuously. He constructed the following self-rating techniques and labeled it:

For My Eyes Only

(See figures 2–5 on pages 32–33.)

1. BEGIN WITH A BANG!

STRENGTHS   AREAS FOR IMPROVEMENT

Figure 2

Ways to Improve This Step

1)_____

2)_____

3)_____

4)_____

2. PLAY TO MY AUDIENCE

STRENGTHS   AREAS FOR IMPROVEMENT

Figure 3

Ways to Improve This Step

1)_____

2)_____

3)_____

4)_____

3. GET 'EM INTO THE ACT

STRENGTHS   AREAS FOR IMPROVEMENT

Figure 4

Ways to Improve This Step

1) _____

2) _____

3) _____

4) _____

4. CLOSE ON CUE

STRENGTHS   AREAS FOR IMPROVEMENT

Figure 5

Ways to Improve This Step

1) _____

2) _____

3) _____

4) _____

8

Bryce Begins to Roll

IT WAS MONDAY MORNING and Bryce was excited. He was sure he "had his act together." He was convinced now that he was ready to take it to the next level. He jotted down the thoughts running through his mind:

"I know that a pro is constantly growing, changing, expanding and serving."

"I know that time can be my greatest asset if I am organized."

"I'm learning to value each appointment, and giving each one my full attention."

"I'm learning that asking and listening aren't enough. That's okay for the semi-pro, but I must truly *hear* in order to help guide my customer in perceiving new possibilities, which he/she may not have thought of previously . When I listen, I am aware of his/her *words*. When I hear, I am aware of his/her *meaning*.

Bryce's first appointment was with Paul Stevenson with Strategic Investments Inc. He had done some personal research and knew that the company was making extensive strategic and tactical plans to manufacture and market a new line of retirement products for the ever expanding retirement planning business. Bryce called a close friend who was a financial planner and learned some interesting and reassuring information about the company's financial posture and position. He had arranged to take a plant tour and complete it in time for his 9:30 time with Mr. Stevenson.

This time, Bryce was prepared to ask substantive, meaningful, and specific questions.

The meeting was cordial. This time Bryce remembered to stress at the outset that he was there for only one major purpose, to help Strategic Investments Inc. meet their quality and profit objectives. Mr. Stevenson was so impressed by Bryce's research and obvious commitment to the success of Strategic Investments that Bryce had to remind himself to ask, listen, and hear if he was indeed going to function at the level of a pro.

As the two talked, Bryce went on to skillfully introduce both features and benefits of the Pinnacle's data management software. Finally, Mr. Stevenson grinned and said, "That works, but what's the total cost?"

When Bryce told him, he seemed to become somewhat strained. "Bryce, I'm sorry, but your price is too high."

Bryce was not really set back by this. Mr. Jackson had told him there'd be moments exactly like this. He had given Bryce a concise summation of techniques used on mathematical reasoning and had added, "Use your intellect, guided by your experience."

The document read like this:

Four Ways to Overcome Price Objections:

+Add: Add up all the benefits a prospective buyer gets from your product or service-the actual tangible values. Add up the *features* that create the benefits. Stress exclusive benefits and features in your discussion.

- Features include:

- Benefits include:

-Subtract: Subtract any features and benefits a prospective buyer *cannot* get in a lower priced product or service. Give extra value to your 'exclusives.' Share the concept that, "I can give you something you want or need that you can't get anywhere else." (Thus creating additional desire)

XMultiply: Multiply by all the intangibles of *quality* and *satisfaction* that your price includes. For example, are prestige and pride of ownership worth anything? They are worth a great deal to most buyers. On some products and services, they are the determining motivation for a sale. The established reputation of what you're selling can be one of the greatest assets in determining fair value. A reputation for *service* and customer satisfaction often influences a buyer's decision to make a higher priced purchase. *This cannot be over-emphasized!*

÷Divide: Divide your price into small units of longer lifetime costs. A $10,000 product, for example, that is guaranteed for five years on parts and service is obviously much more cost-effective than a $7,950 product that is guaranteed for one year. A product that has a maintenance cost of $250 a year after a 10 year period is a better buy than a competitive unit that costs $250 less, but has an average maintenance cost of $1,000 per year over a 10 year period.

=Equals: Take care of your customers and they'll take care of you!

Bryce realized he was not leading Mr. Stevenson through this thought process with excellence, but he did it, and he got the order!

The sale was the largest he had ever closed, and he was beginning to sense that larger orders were more than possible; they were probable, when you function like a pro!

As Bryce headed for his next sales date, he was meeting with Addie Nicholson, purchasing agent for Organic

Opportunities Cafeteria Chain. He decided to stop for lunch and jot down what he was learning about overcoming price objection. The first item to remember, he noted was:

A Rejection=A Dead End

An Objection=An Opportunity

Bryce continued:

1. Most people are *not* price buyers. But nearly everybody is a *value* buyer.

2. Price means absolutely nothing until you know what's being *offered* for sale.

3. Until you've created desire in the customer's mind, the lowest price in the world won't make a sale.

4. In today's competitive world, either a price is right or the seller soon goes out of business. Every sales person *tries* to be competitive.

5. First, you sell the desirability of your product or service; *then* you sell the rightness of your price.

6. The statement that, "Your price is too high" doesn't always mean what it says. It can indicate one of four things:

   a. A need for more information and reassurance.

   b. A desire to buy, but a desire for price justification.

   c. A desire for a cost analysis that translates price into costs.

   d. A genuine belief that your price is too high or an attempt to find out if your price *could* be lower.

7. There are four techniques for overcoming price objections: addition, subtraction, multiplication, and division.

8. Unless you, yourself, believe your price is right, you'll

have a hard time selling it.

9. Keep price in its proper place in your sales presentation.

10. Once you cut prices, your lowest price soon becomes your highest.

11. The price chiseler respects the sales professional that he/she can't chisel: he/she has no respect for the amateur he/she can get to cut a price.

12. Once you cut a price to a customer, he/she has no way of ever knowing for sure that they're getting your lowest price.

13. The sales professional selling the low, middle, and top price ranges all think theirs is the most difficult price justification job.

14. The sales professional who accepts the statement, "your price is too high" without challenging it does more in the long run to reduce prices than the worst price chiseler.

15. The Tough-Minded pro approaches price objections with the "Three D's," dedication, discipline, and determination.

16. Claims that your price is right don't overcome objections unless they're accompanied by convincing proof.

The meeting with Addie Nicholson went pretty well; Bryce got an order that was significantly larger than in his "amateur" days. But, he knew he had much more to learn. His next meeting with Mr. Jackson was a month away, and he was determined to be a real pro by the time they met again. During the next month Bryce:

1. Discovered that "serve" meant more than he realized. It took extra effort, extra time, extra sensitivity, but it paid off and it became a pleasure.

2. Began to follow-up with notes and phone calls to ask how he could serve better. He invited new ideas and really listened. Above all, he heard!

3. He was just beginning to get a whiff of what Mr. Jackson had meant by "beauty and truth." There was something deeply satisfying about knowing he really *cared* and gave every customer his best. He slept more deeply at night than he ever had before. He felt good.

4. He began to go that extra mile and spend an extra hour because it gave him a growing feeling of satisfaction.

5. He began to discover what "honor your customer" really meant. He had originally thought that called for telling the customer whatever they wanted to hear. Now he was beginning to feel that the better he helped his customers feel, the better he felt.

6. He began to realize for the first time that the old phrase, "The shortest distance between two points is a straight line," was an absolute truth. It meant that when your eyes, mind, and spirit are focused on clear goals, you don't go off on tangents and waste time, energy, and effort.

A few days before Bryce was to meet with Mr. Jackson again, he received a phone call explaining that Mr. Jackson was being called out of the country on an urgent consulting engagement. Mr. Jackson's assistant asked if they could make a new appointment for one month later. Bryce agreed and kept on working and experimenting. As a result, his batting average climbed steadily.

At work, the Vice President of Sales commented on the dramatic change in both his production and his appearance. Bryce's numbers had more than doubled, and he was taking more pride in his daily appearance than ever before. As a result, Bryce was asked if he would give a series of presentations to the new sales people who had just come aboard.

Bryce was very tempted to agree to do so, but something told him he wasn't quite ready, so he said, "Thanks for that opportunity, but I'm not quite ready. I will be soon though." Bryce kept on working, selling, and growing.

When he next met with Mr. Jackson he said, "I'm really doing great, but I still don't feel my close rate is all that it could be. Could you give me some real specifics for closing?"

Mr. Jackson nodded and said, "Here are five techniques for closing. They're all you'll ever need if you understand and apply everything else we've been sharing. I didn't give you these techniques at the outset because you simply weren't ready. You needed to learn both the mechanics and dynamics of closing to be a real pro. So, remember, Bryce, these five techniques will only yield excellence if you constantly review and practice all of the other things we've been discussing.

"I'll do it," Bryce said enthusiastically, "just please share those techniques."

"Alright, Bryce. You got it! Before we begin on these five techniques, I'd better say that in actuality, there are many, many ways to close. These five techniques, when mastered, will help insure that you function like a true pro! Later on we'll discuss techniques for functioning and selling at the level of *art*, or how to be a *sales artist*. Such people are rare, but I'm now convinced that you can get there.

In the meantime, here are those five techniques I promised you:

1. *The "Direct Approach"*—There is something real, honest and disarming about coming right out with a request for an order, but only if you've:

   a. Done your homework and research.

    b. Asked about wants, needs, and possibilities.

    c. Listened to wants, needs, and possibilities.

    d. Heard the wants, needs, and possibilities.

"Sometimes a warm demeanor and a frank manner are very effective and you really can say something like, 'You know you're going to buy, so let's decide *how much* and *when,* right now.'

"This approach, of course, requires a lot of sensitivity, caring, and an excellent relationship built on trust.

2. *"The 'Take-It-For-Granted' Technique*—This approach also reflects the sales-pro's confidence. It uses approaches such as, 'Since we're in agreement on everything, when do you want delivery?' or, 'Since we know what you really need, (or want) we might as well start this order rolling-will you sign here please?' or, 'If you decide now, we can customize this and deliver it by. . .' It assumes from what has transpired that a sale has been made, and starts to settle the *customized* details such as quantity, quality, special features, style and delivery dates. This approach is only maximally effective when used with care, empathy and a genuine commitment to a wise decision by the customer.

3. *"The "Either/or" Technique*—This is a powerful closer if you are really thinking and really tuned into the individuality of the customer. For instance, 'As I've shown you, this comes in red or black. The two colors are a toss-up in popularity. Which color do you want to order?' This technique gives the customer a positive *choice* between two alternatives—a choice of style, delivery date, quantity, and price range, etc. When the customer answers the question, he/she has committed himself/herself to an order. Either choice should be attractive to the customer, with their answer depending

on their personal preference.

4. *"The "Step-by-Step" Technique*—(Mr. Jackson's favorite) is virtually irresistible if carried out well enough. This approach can only be done with excellence when you've learned the enormous difference between *expective* and *directive* thinking, words and techniques. Remember the directive person can never truly persuade, they only push. The expective pro truly leads. This technique works amazingly well when you've honed and refined it. It achieves the hard-to-get answer by a series of easy answers and is often the best technique to use with a prospective buyer who hates to make major decisions!

   "For example: 'This corner looks like a good location, do (not don't) you agree? And in this location, I think the intermediate size would be best. Would (not wouldn't) that be your choice? Since it's a rather dark corner, I'd favor the white finish, would you? Installation will take two full days; I'd say we would make shipment to arrive here on Friday so installation can be done over the weekend, to avoid any possible disruption of business. Should we aim for next Friday?'

   Note: This approach requires and uses all the knowledge we have shared to date.

5. *"The "Positive-Negative" Technique*—This approach makes positive use of a negative point which the sales pro knows doesn't apply. In starting with the negative point, the salesperson is certain the customer will refute it, and doing so, suggests the positive point which then becomes the basis for the close.

   For example, the auto sales pro who "confesses" his/her equipment was really not intended for the job you are discussing, but, can be of great assistance in another project that has been previously discussed, which is their intention. In essence, they are identifying possibilities for the customer and identifying how their products fit those possibilities.

Note: It is absolutely critical that no deception takes place in using this technique. Solemn, rigid and humorless use of this technique becomes a manipulative and potentially dishonest approach. Used with humor and cordiality, it can be both effective and profitable."

Mr. Jackson stood up, walked over to a bookshelf and said calmly, "Well, Bryce, how do you feel?"

Bryce looked up intently and said, "I can't wait for my next conversation with a customer!"

9

From Peddler to Pro

IN THE DAYS THAT followed, Bryce seemed to live at the cutting edge of excitement and growth. Every day was an adventure, a new series of experimentations, as well as some trial and error. He seemed to be learning constantly. As he became increasingly open emotionally, he was no longer screening and filtering out the kind of experiences from which he could learn, change, and grow. He discovered for the first time that he had never really been "in charge" or "in control" of a sales appointment when he used to pitch a customer or do too much of the talking.

Now he was noticing that by making an earnest and sincere effort to truly get to know the customer's wants, needs, and possibilities, he could almost always sense precisely *when* and *how* to *close*. He was truly in charge because he *led* and *developed* the whole course of the conversation through his caring, warm, and searching questions.

In his efforts to broaden his reading and learning habits, he began to see solid, satisfying evidence that you really do "become rich in your wallet when you become rich in your mind." Bryce continued to grow, and eagerly anticipated his next meeting with Mr. Jackson.

"Bryce, you look amazingly prosperous and happy," Mr. Jackson said with enthusiasm. "How's it been going?"

Bryce looked pensive for a moment, and then smiled broadly. "You know, I'm pretty sure I've become a full-fledged pro because of an experience I had yesterday, would you like to hear about it?"

Mr. Jackson's eyes lit up. "Absolutely! Let's hear it Bryce."

"It all began months ago when I began to give myself all kinds of excuses to keep from calling on old Matt Kocack who, everybody said, was a sour, hard old boy who had built International Shipping Solutions from the ground up. He, supposedly, ate young sales professionals for breakfast and seemed to enjoy "throwing them out" as he called it.

"I knew I had to find out how professional I had become. I not only wanted to use my new strengths but, as you had suggested, I wanted to find out what strengths I still needed and how I could better use the strengths I now had." Bryce paused.

"Yes, go on, I'm really interested in what happened," Mr. Jackson said intently.

Bryce took a deep breath and went on. "It all began when I called his assistant and indicated how much I was looking forward to getting to know some of the qualities I was sure Mr. Kocack had. She paused on the phone and asked if I was talking about the right Matt Kocack? I assured her I was, and that I was looking forward with real eagerness to getting acquainted. She was gone from the phone for what seemed to be a very, very long time, and when she returned, she told me in a tone which seemed to reflect some slight puzzlement that he would see me the next morning.

"As I drove out to his plant yesterday morning, I was really pretty surprised to discover that I was feeling no anxiety or trepidation. I was really eager to meet him." Bryce paused and then resumed. "You have helped me so very much in changing my view of people. You've said that everyone is an exciting bundle of possibilities, uniqueness, and even potential beauty if we look, think, and *listen* hard enough.

"I was absolutely determined to find some positives and hidden realities in Mr. Kocack. When we met he scowled at me somewhat uncertainly. I wondered immediately if this big, sour-looking man had ever been helped to feel valued, listened to, or really respected. At the outset, he seemed brisk and terse and ready to make our conversation short. However, I really zeroed in on him and I believe my questions reflected some interest in his wants, his particular need, and his possibilities as a businessman and as a total person.

"When he perceived that I was sincere, that I really cared, I could see him begin to relax. More color came into his face; his voice became fuller and lost its dry and semi-sarcastic qualities. After a little while I was pleased to discover, as you'd counseled me, that I was doing most of the listening and Mr. Kocack was doing most of the talking.

"I led him into a discussion of his dream for the company and for his family. He said he'd never found it easy to build a sense of trust with any sales professionals before. We were moving onto a basis of shared meaning and shared understanding.

"I just would not have fully believed the power and practicality of these tools you have given me if I had not seen it with my own eyes.

"I asked, listened, and heard.

"I let myself out and let him in.

"I developed, felt, and showed real interest.

"It became clear to him that I saw some significance in him, not just as a potential customer, but as a real person.

"I wanted to honor him as a customer and as a total person.

"I expected to close an order, and I did.

"I further validated what you have taught, 'The more you give, the more you receive.'

"I found that knowing his dreams led to knowing his goals, objectives, and motives.

"I perceived that my wanting to know about him and his company led to a desire on his part to know more about me and my products. Then, of course, my product knowledge and homework paid off.

"Perhaps, the most insightful and maturing insight I arrived at," (Bryce said slowly and thoughtfully), "was that the chief reason many people seem forbidding, inaccessible, or just plain difficult, is that they are usually lacking adequate self-esteem, confidence, purpose, or direction. They simply don't know how to be open so that they can build a rich chemistry with others. They live behind a mask, or a façade of insecurity. The people whose faces reflect these qualities are the very individuals who need the understanding, reinforcement, and service of people like you and me."

Mr. Jackson whistled softly, "You certainly have made some quantum leaps in growth, but tell me, what happened by the time you walked out of his office?"

"I asked for the order, and got it. The biggest sale of my career!" Bryce grinned. "Additionally, Matt and I have acquired a new friend. I'm going to give him the kind of service and follow-up like I couldn't even visualize a few months ago. It's a great feeling to *know* you're a pro!"

A thoughtful silence ensued. Then Bryce stirred and said, "Will we be meeting again?"

Mr. Jackson looked pleased and said, "That's up to you. I know Mr. Sanchez is so pleased with you, he's encouraged me to work with you as long as your choose."

Bryce inquired, "Well, is there anywhere to go in selling after you become a pro?"

"There is," Mr. Jackson responded, "there is a place on the mountain top. It is the highest level of all. The number of people who have reached this level are few, but they are singularly blessed. Do *you* have the courage to go beyond the profession of selling to the level of *art*? Do you care enough about living a great life to become a sales artist?"

Bryce reflected for only a moment and said firmly, "I do."

10

From Pro to Artist

"THE ART OF SALES is distinguished from craft and profession principally by the sheer amount of creative thought needed." Mr. Jackson grinned, "That's about the first time I've gone academic on you, Bryce, but I thought we needed a lean, clean, definition to build on. Remember, then, that *creative* thought and action are what we are zeroing in on. The word "consultative" has become a buzz word for describing the most advanced and effective form of selling, but I'm afraid most people have only a very limited notion of what is required to move beyond the current stereotypes which seem to define how they can and should feel about other people.

"There is a level of personal and interactive effectiveness experienced by few. While the *pro* is highly self-actualized, the persuasive *artist* goes beyond even that. He or she reaches a level we might call co-actualization.

"The person who functions at this level has gained true insight into key and crucial processes like:

- Shared Meaning—Shared Understanding = Effective

Communication

- Symbiosis

- Synergy

- Cybernetics"

Bryce gave pause, "Hold it a minute that's a bundle at one time, what do they mean?"

"I'm coming to that, Bryce. These things are so important I'd like to make sure I define them carefully. They're powerful!

"First, notice that 'Shared meaning-Shared Understanding' means exactly *that*. You see, if we think of real communication as only dialogue where one person transmits, the other person receives, and vice versa, this is a static concept. To truly *share* means that the communicator is sensitive and empathic. It can develop a similar level of sensitivity and empathy in others by the sheer quality of caring, and thus, sharing. This results in a kind of *simultaneous* comprehension of feelings and insights.

"For example, Bryce, when you are having conversation with a client, ask leading questions that seek out what his/her best interests are. Questions such as, 'What I'm hearing from you is . . .' or, 'Since this topic is a significant concern of yours, have you considered taking a different approach?' 'What are your dreams and goals for your company, your department or your position?'"

Mr. Jackson continued, "Symbiosis means, 'A mutual interdependence between persons or beings.' This means, Bryce, that the true *artist* does such a thorough and caring job of projecting their commitment to the client that, in reality, they feel their own success, joy, and fulfillment is inextricably bound to the feelings and needs in the client. In the Aramaic language, 'self' means that 'sum of you, me, and God.' Or to put it another way, the more you enable the other person to discover and experience their own self-actualization, the more 'synergy' you produce. Synergy is one, and one equals three or more. The whole is indeed greater than the sum of its parts. One of the most potent ways we enable and cause this to happen between people is:

"Confidence + Emotional Vulnerability = Shared feelings of actualization.

"Thus, when we let other people in, emotionally, and let ourselves out, emotionally, true synergy can happen. So when you are on a sales appointment, Bryce, think about putting the emotions, needs, and wants of the client paramount to anything else. Don't be afraid to be yourself, be professional and genuine, but be yourself. Allow the client's best interests in and seek productive, positive solutions in conjunction with the client.

"Does that make sense, Bryce?" Said Mr. Jackson with a wry smile.

"Where to begin," Bryce said, nodding contemplatively. "How do I use these concepts and this knowledge?"

As they began to talk, Mr. Jackson turned to a wall chart showing four levels of human development. It was called:

Batten's Continuum of Actualization

The Possible Dream

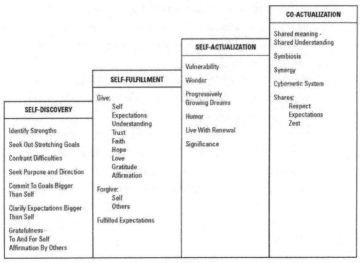

BATTEN'S CONTINUUM OF ACTUALIZATION
- THE POSSIBLE DREAM -

SELF-DISCOVERY	SELF-FULFILLMENT	SELF-ACTUALIZATION	CO-ACTUALIZATION
			Shared meaning - Shared Understanding
			Symbiosis
		Vulnerability	Synergy
	Give:	Wonder	Cybernetic System
	Self	Progressively	Shares:
Identify Strengths	Expectations	Growing Dreams	Respect
	Understanding	Humor	Expectations
Seek Out Stretching Goals	Trust	Live With Renewal	Zest
	Faith	Significance	
Confront Difficulties	Hope		
Seek Purpose and Direction	Love		
	Gratitude		
Commit To Goals Bigger	Affirmation		
Than Self			
	Forgive:		
Clarify Expectations Bigger	Self		
Than Self	Others		
Gratefulness -	Fulfilled Expectations		
To And For Self			
Affirmation By Others			

Figure 6

As the session ended, Bryce was confident he wanted become an artist. Since it was Friday evening, Bryce had time to do a lot of thinking over the weekend. "Can a person really care, share, and dare that much?" He wondered.

Bryce's wife Samantha had witnessed a change in her husband, his thought processes, his confidence level, the way he dressed throughout the process. Bryce's entire demeanor was evolving. She encouraged him to practice with her as he role-played through what Mr. Jackson had shared.

Together they talked, explored and shared their growing insight.

On Monday morning, Bryce set out to keep the appointment he'd made with Ashley Donovan, the President of RESULTS, Inc. He felt ready.

From the moment Bryce entered the reception area of RESULTS, he knew this was going to be a different type of experience, with a more positive result. He was just starting to get the sense of what it felt like to *give, care* and *serve.* Bryce was absolutely convinced that his line, Pinnacle Products, were exactly what RESULTS, Inc. needed to help them reach their organizational goals. He didn't really know why or *how* yet, but he was ready for the challenge of asking, listening, hearing and leading Ms. Donovan to new insights and possibilities.

Bryce found himself wondering, "Do physicians, clergymen, or professors have as many opportunities as a sales artist to truly use their talents in ways that could potentially enrich and fulfill the lives of others?"

As he reflected on their last meeting, Mr. Jackson had exuded energy when he discussed living, working and *persuading* at the level of art. His face had become luminous as he'd said:

The persuasive sales artist goes beyond self-actualization to co-actualization. That is, he/she not only experiences the enthusiasm and prosperity which derives from serving others superbly, he/she helps them develop the desire and capacity to become fully actualized themselves.

Bryce remembered saying, "Yeah, I see. In other words you have reached a point where just helping me grow and succeed, therefore actualizing you, is not enough. In addition to this, you are committed to helping me discover the personal impact of actualizing others."

After this statement, Mr. Jackson had grinned ear to ear and said, "You got it, Bryce!"

"Right this way, Mr. Norman." Ms. Donovan's assistant was asking Bryce to follow her to the President's office.

As Ms. Donovan held out her hand, Bryce was acutely aware that the difference between a Pro (even though there aren't enough of them) and a sales-artist was going to require much more than theory. Here was an opportunity, here was a challenge, here were wants, needs, and possibilities, and the time was *now*.

On the way over Bryce had reviewed and reflected on the distinction Mr. Jackson had drawn between the Pro and the Artist.

Pros function pretty consistently at the level of excellence. They are members of that rare group that live up to most of their possibilities and actualize their own talents and dreams. They prosper!

Bryce had, by now, a whiff of that fine feeling of sales success. The definition of the artist, however, was significantly different, considerably more stretching. He began to reflect upon Mr. Jackson's wisdom, "Ask, listen and hear to determine wants, needs and possibilities." Bryce thought, "This can't be the status quo sales conversation, I need to invest myself in helping RESULTS, Inc. exceed their goals through my services. I need to *ask* questions, seek clarification on her answers, and help her discover *possibilities* for RESULTS, Inc."

Ashley Donovan seemed to sense Bryce's enthusiasm and dedication to her company's vision, mission and values. (It should be noted that a new and different aura and presence is developed and projected when one reaches Bryce's level. In an almost metaphysical manner, others seem to sense not only the absence of threat, but the presence of affirmation and reaffirmation, of assurance and reassurance. They can relax, think acutely, and make major decisions.)

Bryce began asking questions. "Where do you see your company six months, twelve months, and three years from now? What are your major organizational strengths? What are you most concerned about, and how can we best help you fill that gap? What are your dreams for RESULTS?"

As Bryce asked, listened and flexibly and caringly *heard* about the wants, needs and possibilities of Ms. Donovan, a pattern something like this emerged:

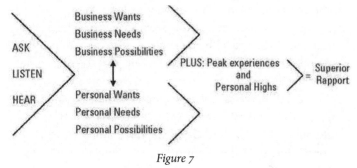

Figure 7

Because of Bryce's positive, open aura, Ashley was able to relax, think acutely, and make effective decisions. Bryce continued, "I can't tell you how much I appreciate all the information you've been sharing with me, Ms. Donovan. Your dreams for the company and your family certainly demonstrate that you're a person who *cares* a lot about a great many things." Bryce continued to ask more about the company's vision, mission and values, about long-term possibilities for the RESULTS, and about how Pinnacle could help Ms. Donovan and her company reach and exceed these benchmarks.

Bryce prompted her by *asking* her, "Where, specifically, do you want RESULTS to be in six months, Ms. Donovan?" "How can we partner to help you reach your goals?"

Ashley Donovan contemplated for a minute and then reached behind a filing cabinet and pulled out a "vision board" for RESULTS Inc. She had cut pictures from different magazines, newspapers, and advertisements that represented goals for herself and her company. Ms. Donovan proceeded to detail each one. The arrow facing upwards represented increasing notoriety within the business community, the yellow smiley face represented employee morale, and the picture of blueprints represented her dreams for RESULTS Inc. Bryce smiled and asked, "Will you work with me to achieve these goals?"

Ms. Donovan said, "You seem to be truly interested in the business plans, the company's future, and in providing options for how we can reach our goals. You seem to legitimately care."

"I do," Bryce said simply (and he meant it), and then went about skillfully leading Ms. Donovan through a process much like that shown in the illustration below. They worked on establishing priorities, goals, dreams, and what the next logical steps for RESULTS could look like. Ashley paused, taking notes; she was finding new and different

KEY ELEMENTS OF THE CONSULTATIVE PRESENTATION FOR THE "SALES ARTIST" OF TODAY AND TOMORROW

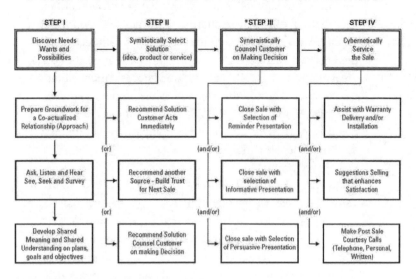

*The artist stays loose and flexible about <u>when</u> to ASK FOR THE ORDER.
The artist senses, emphasizes, seeks and cares, thus knows the "optimum moment" to ASK.

Figure 8

56

When their conversation drew to a close, several things had happened:

1. They had set four dates to meet in the future for the purpose of evaluating the profit posture and progress of RESULTS, Inc., and the further clarification and implementation of Ms. Donovan's new commitment to be a truly people-oriented leader. She was beginning to subscribe to Bryce's system that good management is of, by, about and for *people*.

2. Bryce had closed the largest sale of his career.

3. A new friendship was formed

4. Bryce identified new possibilities, assigned dates and deadlines, and set them in motion.

5. He had gained a whiff of a future beyond all of his past ideas.

6. Most importantly, Bryce was learning *how to exceed himself through service to others*!

That evening as he walked up the steps to his home with quickening strides, Samantha pulled in the driveway behind him and called out, "So, how did your sales go today?"

Bryce relaxed, smiled and said, "I closed the biggest sale of my career! When I got back to the office, Clayton Sanchez, our CEO, had left me a personalized note of congratulations. I think they're starting to notice me more at the office!"

Samantha replied, "I really expected it; your appearance, confidence and attitude towards others is so drastically different. You really have a presence now, and you are more engaged with our family."

That evening Bryce touched base with Mr. Jackson on the phone and said, "Tomorrow I have a date with Jim Best,

President of Capital, Ltd. I'll be the fifth and final representative he's talking to before he makes the decision on who gets all of Capital's business. I plan to invest myself in truly learning their business and needs, and when I've landed this one, I believe I will be taking steps towards becoming a true *artist*."

"Go to it, Bryce," said Mr. Jackson, "Just remember to ask, listen and hear to determine the wants, needs, and possibilities of the client. Remember to be positive, ask questions, and truly *hear* what is best for Capital and Mr. Best. I know you can do it my friend."

"What approach could I take to build a strong rapport with Mr. Best?" asked Bryce.

"Ask for his dreams, provide options, and combine your knowledge with theirs to create synergy. Brainstorm possibilities, build on strengths, have an open, honest demeanor, exude true confidence (which means also being open) and *expect the best,* Bryce!"

Before going to bed, Bryce again reviewed some important words. Research at Harvard had revealed these words were tested and proven to be effective in persuasion:

You	*Advantage*
Save	Guarantee
Money	Security
Health	Discovery
Easy	*New*
Now	*Benefit*
Safety	*Positive*
Results	Proven

He was beginning to discover for himself that the words in *italics* were the most effective of all. As he switched off the light, two words were going through his mind over and over. They were—care, serve, care, serve, care, serve,

The date with Jim Best posed fresh challenges. Mr. Best had recently led a seminar on "How to Negotiate" and he saw every face-to-face business situation as a challenge to get ahead of the other person

With his newly awakened and sharpened senses, Bryce soon diagnosed the appropriate approach.

This was made possible because he had already started rolling with his new Modus Operandi.

- He had researched the company and Mr. Best.

- He had approached the date with a commitment to care and serve.

- He kept remembering that 80% of all sales are made by the 20% who care enough.

- He asked, listened, and heard in order to determine wants, needs, and possibilities.

- He caringly related to the goals and dreams of Mr. Best.

- His total aura and presence emanated *warmth* and *trust*.

He had done, and was doing these things, but still sensed a certain defensiveness from Mr. Best. Then he remembered yet another of Mr. Jackson's wise thoughts:

If your customer seems at all guarded, defensive, or apprehensive, make very sure that you are not that way yourself. Vulnerability begets vulnerability. Weakness and defensiveness beget weakness and defensiveness. In contrast, vulnerability fueled by confidence is unstoppable.

He said, "Mr. Best, please search your mind and ask me anything and everything about our products and your wishes you can possibly think of. We must have no secrets—no hidden agendas. If you are in any way dubious about our quality, our pricing, our service, or our follow through, please say so. We know we aren't perfect but the only way we'll be the really excellent company, is to know fully what keen and seasoned business people like you think, want, and need. For instance, this line of valves . . ."

He went on drawing Mr. Best out until, for the first time, he truly understood Mr. Jackson's counsel to diffuse, de-fuse, and dissolve defenses. His heart actually began to beat more rapidly when he realized he now had a hands-on feel of the final major principle he had been seeking:

The greatest deterrent to closing a sale is defensiveness fueled by something less than total trust.

Therefore . . .

The greatest power to build superb sales and relationships is the power to build a relationship of total trust continuously fueled by competence and integrity.

It was through this final principle that Bryce learned the importance of social capital, or the ability to build multiple, positive, trustworthy relationships that serve as assets to your personal and professional life, as you serve as an asset to these individuals.

A thought rushed through Bryce's head:

Trust + Honor + Integrity + Service=Social Capital (positive, trustworthy, relationships that serve as symbiotic assets to both parties)

As the meeting came to a close Bryce asked, "Can we consider this a done deal, Mr. Best? As a client and partner of Pinnacle, I will personally ensure we are exceeding your expectations."

Bryce walked out with Mr. Best's assurance that Capital, Ltd. would be buying *all* of their production and engineering supplies from him. Mr. Best's voice seemed to resonate in his ears and he felt as though he was on top of the world.

He knew he had grown at an astonishing rate as a total person. He was experiencing a sharp increase in income and personal satisfaction. Samantha and the children were returning the kind of caring and supportive glow he was projecting.

Bryce knew there'd be days when he didn't feel the greatest. He knew there'd be challenges and barriers ahead from time to time because life is real and life is earnest. However, now he knew he could grow from these challenges, and he had the tools to face them head on. He knew he would savor the flavor of being a *winner* in every aspect of his life.

11

The New Mentor

WEEKS FLEW BY FOR Bryce, and he was still in awe of how his professional and personal life had done a complete 180 over the last several months. He was growing as a total person both on and off the job. He got more involved in church, volunteer committees, and his children's school. Soon he began to get calls and messages asking him for "advice." Even now, he'd reflect upon counsel Mr. Jackson had shared.

Bryce thought:

Advice is telling people what they should do.

But . . .

Counsel is helping people determine for *themselves* what to *be* and *do*, in that order.

As he succeeded week by week in putting together closer and closer intervals of excellence, he coined a phrase which he felt was a worthwhile parallel for a sales *artist*. He called this individual the *Excellent Persuader*.

Bryce had no intention of leaving the Pinnacle Company right now. He had however been given the opportunity to coach others and lead new staff trainings for the sales department. The requests for Bryce's counsel continued, and he found a great deal of efficacy fitting this into and around his busy schedule.

It had now been close to a year since he had met with Mr. Jackson, and the last correspondence he had with him was a long thank you note and a couple of brief, subsequent phone calls. However, one day, Bryce received a package and a letter from Mr. Jackson. He shared a list of over 250 strengths he identified in Bryce throughout their meetings. Mr. Jackson concluded the letter by saying, ". . . this name plate was especially prepared for you because I feel you truly represent precisely what it says. May you continue to share your gifts with others as they grow, and they surely will."

The name plate said:

Bryce Norman
The Excellent Persuader

Bryce looked pleased, amused, and thoughtful, as he said to Samantha, "That guy never stops growing; he is always committed to excellence!"

She smiled and said, "You've become quite a guy yourself, you know! Do you realize you've become a mentor to a lot of people?"

Bryce was grateful, he knew it was happening. He had realized that being a sales *artist* wasn't strictly about his job, but that every aspect of life pertains to sales. Grant writers, fundraisers, non-profit executives, making acquaintances, a job interview, the first client meeting, these were all sales opportunities, reframed into daily experiences. Bryce determined he wanted to help others realize that through authentic relationships, all individuals can excel in their day-to-day lives!

He leaned back in his chair after Samantha had left and saw a vision.

He visualized a future where men, women, and young people by the thousands, perhaps by the millions, would perceive the sheer practicality of excelling in:

1. Asking, listening, and hearing

2. Building, not destroying

3. Caring, sharing, and daring

4. Cultivating physical, mental, and spiritual health

5. Loving, living, and laughing

6. Being, and then doing

7. Leading, not pushing or driving

8. Asking, not telling

9. Expecting, not directing

10. Expecting the best from all dimensions of life

11. Giving, not getting

12. Building on strengths

13. Relishing synergy

Other power words and phrases from the Masters ran through his mind again and again. Phrases like:

Above all, know thyself.

To thine own self be true.

Before we can do the noble, we must first do the useful.

Sweet are the uses of adversity.

Before we can move the world, we must first find ourselves.

My self is the sum of you, me, and God

He let himself dream further . . .

I will strive for personal and professional excellence at all levels. I will give, not get, and I will write excellence upon the door-posts of my heart.

He knew he could do it.

Will you join him in the challenge?

One Minute Answers to Become an "Excellent Persuader"

Questions Frequently Asked About Becoming an "Excellent Persuader."

1. "Is it possible for me to reach the *artist* level of selling? Is there a chart that shows the steps?"

2. "What is the 'Excellent Persuader's' blueprint for success?"

3. "Does what you wear really matter? I feel most like myself in jeans and a polo."

4. "Oh, come on, a handshake is a handshake, isn't it?"

5. "All I want from that customer is the sale, and he/she should give it to me if I'm first, right?"

6. "I've heard of consultative selling. Could you tell me more about how it works?"

7. "Sure, I ask a lot of questions, but when I think back I guess I never really listen to the answer. Am I missing something?"

8. "Just as an athlete has certain skills to qualify as a pro on the playing field, there must be certain face-to-face skills for me to become an 'Excellent Persuader.' What are they?"

9. "I use an appointment book, but the 'Excellent Persuader' talks about a date book. What is the difference?"

10. "I've heard a lot about goals, but what is goal setting and how does it relate to personal development?"

11. "Sometimes a customer will interrupt my work, is it worth diverging my efforts at that time?

12. "I'm not always proud to tell people I sell for a living. It isn't a career with much clout, is it?"

13. "There are times when I *think* I am a failure because I can't close a particular account or achieve a particular objective. My entire attitude is negatively affected wondering if I'll get the sale. Does this matter?"

14. "So what, I made a sale, what is in it for me, but a little commission?"

15. "I've heard that dedication, discipline, and determination are the corner posts of the sales artist. Could you give me a checklist to see how I measure up?

16. "What is the 'Excellent Persuader's' road map for turning dreams into reality?"

17. "Some people say the power of a question is infinitely stronger than the power of a statement. Can you share some specific types of questions that can be used?"

18. "What is a 'Strength's Notebook' and how do I make one?"

19. "How do I make myself indispensable in the workplace?"

Question: "Is it possible for me to reach the *artist* level of selling? Is there a chart that shows the steps?"

Answer: "*Potential* 'Excellent Persuaders' are to be found at all levels on the pathway to the top in selling. No matter where you are (see illustration below) in the spectrum of self-development—from peddler through craftsman, semi-pro, to pro – if you acquire the skills listed under each level, you will move on to the next level. Ultimately, through this process you will reach the level of artist and become an 'Excellent Persuader.'"

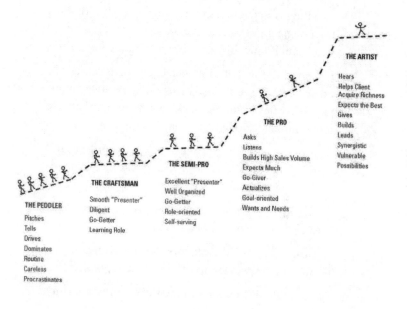

THE ARTIST

Hears
Helps Client
Acquire Richness
Expects the Best
Gives
Builds
Leads
Synergistic
Vulnerable
Possibilities

THE PRO

Asks
Listens
Builds High Sales Volume
Expects Much
Go-Giver
Actualizes
Goal-oriented
Wants and Needs

THE SEMI-PRO

Excellent "Presenter"
Well Organized
Go-Getter
Role-oriented
Self-serving

THE CRAFTSMAN

Smooth "Presenter"
Diligent
Go-Getter
Learning Role

THE PEDDLER

Pitches
Tells
Drives
Dominates
Routine
Careless
Procrastinates

Figure 9

Question: "What is the 'Excellent Persuader's' blueprint for success?"

Answer: "The 'Excellent Persuader's' blueprint for success is summarized in the following 23 points. The "Excellent Persuader:"

1. Knows and sees his/her own present and potential strengths.

2. Has a set of stretching expectations.

3. Is committed to the principles of *service, education, attitude,* and *discipline.*

4. Understands that nothing really happens until somebody sells something, and understands this process of selling is much more than being a peddler, or even than being a pro. It is a level of artistry that the truly successful human being is always trending towards.

5. Perceives the activities associated with meeting another person as a *positive* experience. Positive anticipation creates a "dating-like process" rather than the more mundane activity of making appointments.

6. Knows the value of a "high-touch relationship" and conveys warmth, confidence, and caring in handshakes and other nonverbal cues.

7. Understands the power of a question is infinitely greater than the power of a statement.

8. Realizes that you must ask, listen, and really hear to determine other peoples' wants, needs, and possibilities.

9. Is committed to mutually rewarding relationships with other people, and realizes that to get from others, you must first start by giving to others. The "Excellent Persuader" is a *go-giver* rather than a go-getter.

10. Realizes that the use of one's time will determine the space one acquires in this world.

11. Believes in helping others reach their potential.

12. Understands the power of the A.S.K formula for achieving action in all human endeavors.

    A: *ask and it shall be given*
    S: *seek and you shall find*
    K: *knock and it will be opened unto you*

13. Realizes that you become rich in your wallet by becoming rich in your mind.

14. Understands that everyone is an exciting bundle of possibilities, uniqueness, and potential beauty if we look, think, and listen hard enough.

15. Understands that sales *artist* is a consultant who employs creative thought to bring about co-actualization in the satisfying of needs, wants, and possibilities.

16. Feels exhilarated by the thoughts associated with giving, caring, and serving.

17. Experiences joy by the thought of asking, listening, hearing, and leading others into new insights and possibilities.

18. Realizes that Pros function pretty consistently at the level of excellence. They are members of that rare group that live up to the most of their possibilities, and usually actualize their own talents and dreams.

19. Understands that the persuasive sales artist goes beyond self-actualization to *co-actualization*. They not only experience the energy and prosperity which derives from serving others superbly, they help others develop the desire and capacity to become fully actualized themselves.

20. Realizes that the vocabulary we use has an effect on our thoughts and actions, as well as the thoughts and actions of others; therefore strives to build a speaking and writing vocabulary of positive, powerful words

and eliminates negative, weak words.

21. Understands that weak and defensive behaviors beget weak and defensive behaviors from others; therefore replaces these behaviors with strong, vulnerable, and caring verbal and nonverbal behaviors.

22. Realizes that the greatest deterrent to closing the sale is defensiveness fueled by something less than total trust, therefore the greatest power to build superb sales (and relationships) is the power to build a relationship of total trust, one that is continuously fueled by competence and integrity.

23. Understands that advice is telling people what they should do, but coaching, counseling or consulting is helping people determine for themselves what to be and do (in that order).

Question: "Does what you wear really matter? I feel most like myself in jeans and a polo."

Answer: What you wear should thunder so loud that people will want to hear what you have to say. When you step into a room, even though no one in that room knows you or has seen you before, people will make many decisions about you based solely on your appearance. These decisions supply answers in the following areas:

- Your economic level

- Your educational level

- Your trustworthiness

- Your social position

- Your level of sophistication

- Your economic heritage

- Your success

- Your moral character

To be an "Excellent Persuader" in almost any endeavor, you must be sure that those decisions about you are favorable, because in that first impression you make, you are what you wear.

Question: "Oh, come on, a handshake is a handshake, isn't it?"

Answer: The value of an effective handshake is seldom communicated, on a conscious, rational verbal level. Good or poor handshakes more often are communicated on a non-verbal, subconscious feeling level. The value and power of human contact has long been underestimated. "Excellent Persuaders" realize the value of an appropriate, confident handshake.

These nonverbal, subconscious feelings fit into one of two categories depending upon the quality of the handshake. On a scale of 1 (very poor handshake) to 10 (excellent handshake), the following illustration identifies the subconscious feelings associated with a handshake.

SCALE FOR RATING THE HANDSHAKE

Poor Handshake					Excellent Handshake				
1	2	3	4	5	6	7	8	9	10
Offers:					Offers:				
	aloofness					warmth			
	indifference					concern			
	insecurity					confidence			
	weakness					enthusiasm			

Figure 10

Because the feelings associated with an excellent handshake are so important to serve at the sales artist level, it is important to understand the subconscious criteria used in evaluating the handshake.

The Nonverbal Message in a Handshake

Evaluative Criteria	Poor	Good
Degree of firmness	weak	firm
Degree of dryness	moist	dry
Depth of interlock	grips fingers only	full, deep grip
Duration of grip	very short	moderate
Eye contact	none	maintained throughout handshake

Figure 11

Question: "All I want from that customer is the sale, and he/she should give it to me if I'm first, right?"

Answer: Somewhere and somehow (and many years ago) the idea developed that selling was *making* people buy something for the sole purpose of *getting* some income for the salesperson.

This is possibly the most damaging and outdated idea ever to impact the selling profession. At the very heart of the Hippocratic Oath, and the oath of other professions such as law and education, is the concept of serving.

Now, are you ready for this? *Serving* and *selling* come from the same Latin root word and mean exactly the same prior to translation.

Have you ever met a real pro, a true master of persuasion, an artist at selling? If so, you will invariably note that he/she is a go-giver, not a go-getter. And, he/she will spend much effort focusing on how to better serve the customer. Remember, superior service means superior sales!

Question: "I've heard of consultative selling. Could you tell me more about how it works?"

Answer: Consultative selling:

- Is nothing really new or revolutionary.

- Is the way highly successful salespeople sell; they ask questions and sell solutions.

- Is a way of selling that fits what your prospective clients want and how you work.

- Is not a high pressure type of salesmanship.
  Why prospects turn off:
  They:

- Don't like one-way monologue

- Don't like being dominated or pressured.

- Don't like the focus on what the salesperson wants.

- Don't like to do business with a person who hasn't developed "prospect confidence."
  Why prospects turn on:

- Skillful questioning allows them to discuss problems.

- They feel you recognize and appreciate their wants, needs, and possibilities.

- They agree that your service features meet their needs, wants and possibilities.

- They see benefit to themselves or their company

- They want to work with you because you make them feel significant and important.

Be careful:

You must concern yourself with your client's perception of the benefits of your product or service, not your own. What he/she sees as important *is* important. What you see as important *may* not be important to them. The client may decide to buy for an entirely different reason than the reasons or benefits you expect to impress upon him/her. Your prospect's value system is based on his/her experience and what appeals to him/her, not on what has appeal to you.

Your effective approach:

Question and *develop* facts regarding prospect's values, needs, wants, and their importance to him/her. Develop a relationship of trust, whereby the prospect will look to you for honest counsel. The more trust you engender, the more counsel you elicit, the more listening you do, and the more hearing you engage in, will result in greater receptivity to your proposition.

Question: "Sure, I ask a lot of questions, but when I think back I guess I never really listen to the answer. Am I missing something?"

Answer: At a very early age people are taught to talk. For most people, this became one of their first major accomplishments, and was recognized as such. They went on to school and were further taught to speak, and in turn, recognized for their accomplishments. However, few people were taught to listen!

The "Excellent Persuader" realizes the power of effective talking; however he/she also recognizes the tremendous power there is to be had by asking questions, listening, and really hearing and understanding what others are saying. Extensive research indicates that withheld listening for prolonged periods of time is a form of brainwashing and only serves to block and destroy productive relationships. In fact, many tribes in underdeveloped parts of the world used withheld listening and recognition as a means of punishment. Those so sentenced often go off by themselves and ultimately die.

Consultative artist-level selling is built on a foundation of asking questions and then carefully observing, listening, and really hearing the prospect's response. It is a dialogue, not a monologue that helps create shared meaning and shared understanding (the true definition of communication).

The "Excellent Persuader" also realizes the value of the aforementioned A.S.K. formula. This formula has stood the test of time and is one of the hallmarks of discovering the kind of service one can supply. Again, the formula stands for:

A: ask and it shall be given
S: seek and you shall find
K: knock and it will be opened unto you

The "Excellent Persuader" understands that the wiser person is usually the one who is asking questions and does most of the listening.

Question: "Just as an athlete has certain skills to qualify as a pro on the playing field, there must be certain face to face skills for me to become an 'Excellent Persuader.' What are they?"

Answer: Only amateurs and "small" people live defensively! Who grows when he/she retreats into themselves? Who grows when he/she defends? If a muscle encounters no resistance or healthy stress, it atrophies and dies. The same is true of the mind. We must have challenges and stretching goals. Life without work is a shortcut to deterioration. When we don't have stretching challenges to make our heart beat rapidly, that make our senses quicken, we do not force the blood out to our extremities and we begin to dry up and wither from the outside in.

Please carefully examine the below terminology:

Openness – Would you buy anything valuable from a salesperson whose voice, looks, manner, and personality are closed in and self-serving? Would you? Your customers will undoubtedly feel the same way.

Positive Listening and Hearing – Perhaps the greatest single skill of a pro is to truly listen and hear. If you do everything else excellently, but still listen negatively, this will cancel out just about everything else. Excellent listening diffuses and defuses the defenses of the customer.

Expectations – This is a clear, focused awareness of what you want to happen. When you clarify your expectations, you are setting the stage for all the right things to happen.

Kinesics – The physical and total impression you make on your customer is more important than what you say. It is important to appear:

1. Open and caring

2. Vulnerable

3. Committed to service

4. Calm and controlled

Integrity – Make sure you mean what you *say* and *do*, or don't say and do it. Remember that a promise made is a debt unpaid.

Caring – The amateur (at anything) cares more about self than anything else. The pro thinks first of his/her customer's wants, needs, and possibilities.

Reinforcement – Build the self-esteem of your customer by what you say, do, and are.

Forming Conclusions – If you become skilled in all of these areas you will become increasingly keen and knowledgeable about when to ask for the order. More importantly, you'll begin to become very good at helping the customer move beyond the fulfillment of his/her wants and needs to a discovery of *possibilities.*

FACE TO FACE SKILLS

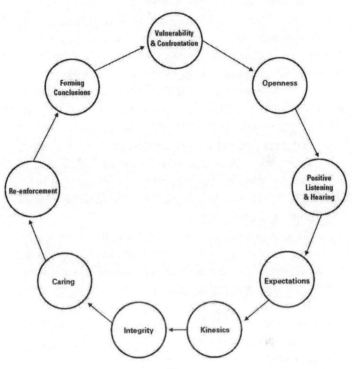

Figure 12

All of the above adds up to *consultative* or *counselor* selling. Some specific techniques of consultative selling are:

1. Become interested in and knowledgeable about the customer's goals, objectives, and operating problems.

2. Become interested in and knowledgeable about the customer's wants, needs, and possibilities.

3. Ask, listen and hear!

Question: "I use an appointment book, but the 'Excellent Persuader' talks about a date book. What is the difference?"

Answer: The "Excellent Persuader" turns his/her appointment book into a datebook. With this name change he/she also changes his/her attitude toward one of anticipation, expectation, caring, sharing and serving. One is not flirting, simply putting forth their best at all times.

At the end of each week the "Excellent Persuader" finds a quiet spot to study the past week's activities associated with his/her datebook. Each of the sales dates are studied reviewing strengths and weaknesses of his/her communication. From this analysis he/she makes a list of ways that would have made each of the conversations more effective. This list becomes a goal sheet for the development of future strengths.

The goal sheet for developing strengths is carried with the "Excellent Persuader" until such time as needed to build this strength into the subconscious mind. Modern medical research indicates that it takes about 30 days of thinking, feeling, talking, and practicing for a new habit to replace an old one. As each of these strengths becomes a habit, the "Excellent Persuader" moves one step closer to becoming a *sales artist*.

Question: "I've heard a lot about goals, but what is goal setting and how does it relate to personal development?"

Answer: Unused iron grows rusty. Stagnant water becomes murky. Airplanes rust out faster on the ground than in the air. Humans who don't use their God-given talents lose them! Because of the "use it or lose it" truth about life, it is imperative to have a personal list of stretching expectations about self for self-development.

The "Excellent Persuader" realizes he/she is a bundle of potentialities that are waiting to be developed into actualities of strengths. The difference between your perceived potentiality and your current actuality is equal to your expectation/goal. The "Excellent Persuader" has clearly defined goals that will develop strengths into future actualities.

Goals or expectations stretch people from their current actuality toward their potentiality. Modern biology, medicine, psychology, philosophy, and religion are increasingly discovering that healthy, happy, productive, and successful people are always moving toward their potentialities. These individuals are growing—not static, supple—not rigid, open—not closed, vibrant—not lethargic. The reason for this is that they are continually stretching themselves toward the development of their strengths with stretching goals.

Goals should be set on a daily basis with daily to-do lists. Monthly goals should be set and carried with oneself where they will be a constant reminder. Yearly goals should be set and placed where one will see them at least twice a day, preferably at least once in the morning and once in the evening. One suggestion for placement of annual goals is to print them on an adhesive-backed paper and place them on the inside of your billfold or dashboard (see illustrations).

Long-term goals for the next five, ten, and fifteen years should also be set. These can be developed in the form of a vision board, and are most effective when framed and hung in a private office, den, or bedroom.

My 30-Day Goals

By _____ 20____ I will

1) _____

_____

(Personal Goal)

2) _____

_____

(Family Goal)

3) _____

_____

(Business Goals)

Date **1-13-08**

DAILY TO-DO LIST

Priority	Items to do
3	— Call Houston Motors to check on installation of copy machine
2	— Call Price Optical to make an appointment for product demonstration
4	— Attend Chamber of Commerce 3:00 P.M.
1	— Call Simmons Furniture and deal with customer complaint

Notes for tomorrow:

Figure 13

Daily Schedule	
8:00 A.M. (1½ hrs.)	Check into office Handle all paper work. (New listings, correspondence, filling, preparation of advertising, etc.)
9:30 A.M. (1 hr.)	Telephone contacts for new listings (Expired listings, previous clients, etc.)
10:30 A.M. (1½ hrs.)	Contact with current listings, current sales, buyer loan appliances, etc.
12:00 Noon	Lunch
1:00 P.M. (1½ hrs.)	Inspect potential listings that you have contacted by phone or have been referred to.
2:30 P.M. (2 hrs.)	Showings to prospective buyers - When no appointments to show, call prospects and arrange showings on other days.
4:30 P.M. (1 hr.)	Attend closings of sales, handling of misc. details, planning next day's schedule.
Evening	Showing property and securing listings as client's time may require.

Two Week Appointment Schedule
Microcomputer Sales Representative

Mon.	Tues.	Wed.	Thurs.	Fri.	Sat.-Sun.
10:30 Wheat First Searches 12:00 Lunch with Ray Williams 3:00 Darrelle Service Center	9:00 Demonstration at Chester Festival 11:00 Demo at Mills Inc. 3:30 Meet with Helen Sisson	9:00 Sales Mtg. at Imperial Moose Lodge 1:30 Demo at Omega Homes	9:30 Park Realty 11:00 White Tire Service 2:00 Demo at Ritter Seafood	9:00 Austin & Son Storage 10:30 Demo at CMP Sporting Goods 1:00 Attend Computer Trade Show	

Mon.	Tues.	Wed.	Thurs.	Fri.	Sat.-Sun.

Figure 14

Building Versus Destroying Customer Relations

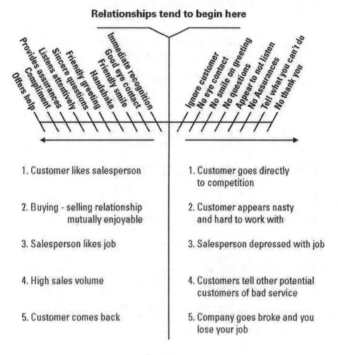

Relationships tend to begin here

Offers help
Provides assurances
Listens attentively
Sincere questions
Friendly greeting
Handshake
Immediate recognition
Good eye contact
Friendly smile
Compliment

Ignore customer
No eye contact
No smile on greeting
No questions
Appear to not listen
No Assurances
Tell what you can't do
No thank you

1. Customer likes salesperson	1. Customer goes directly to competition
2. Buying - selling relationship mutually enjoyable	2. Customer appears nasty and hard to work with
3. Salesperson likes job	3. Salesperson depressed with job
4. High sales volume	4. Customers tell other potential customers of bad service
5. Customer comes back	5. Company goes broke and you lose your job

Figure 15

Question: "Sometimes a customer will interrupt my work. Is it worth diverging my efforts at that time?"

Answer: The "Excellent Persuader" understands that relationships can be fragile. He/she is proactive rather than reactive and realizes how important his/her verbal and non-verbal actions are in developing synergistic, co-actualized relationships.

The table on the following page illustrates verbal and nonverbal behaviors that have a significant effect on the quality and outcomes of a relationship.

Question: "I'm not always proud to tell people I sell for a living. It isn't a career with much clout, is it?"

Answer: The skills of the "Excellent Persuader" can be applied to *all* fields where communication is important (see illustration below). Robert Louis Stevenson wrote, "Everybody lives by selling something!" Charles Schwab said, "We are all salespeople every day of our lives, selling our ideas and enthusiasm to those with whom we come in contact!" Calvin Coolidge said in a broad, generic sense that, "Without salespeople there would never have been a United States of America!"

Today we live in an *information-oriented economy and society*. More people work in careers where information is the commodity provided than ever before. The effective exchange of information (communication = shared meaning, shared understanding) becomes the bottom line for measuring performance and productivity.

The attorney who communicates effectively and persuasively with both the client and adversary will be providing improved productivity and *performance*. Soon large numbers of clients will be seeking this individual out. The medical doctor must have good doctor/patient relationships, be skillful at diagnosing needs, wants and possibilities, and be effective at communicating a proper solution to the patient. These are skills used by the "Excellent Persuader."

Remember:

Trust + Honor + Integrity + Service=Social Capital (positive, trustworthy, relationships that serve as symbiotic assets to both parties)

The "Excellent Persuader" is based around the philosophies of great leaders of the past. They were more visionary than likely anticipated because the skills of the "Excellent Persuader" are more important in today's society than ever before.

Question: "There are times when I *think* I am a failure because I can't close a particular account or achieve a particular objective. My entire attitude is negatively affected wondering if I'll get the sale. Does this matter?"

Answer: The single greatest breakthrough in human growth and development has been the discovery that you "become what you think." *You* are the *sum* of your *attitudes*. The mind grows and becomes resilient and tough only through use. It atrophies through idleness and ease. The most effective minds are those which have been invigorated by practical experiences and challenges.

Please think through and complete the following by placing a check mark where you are now:

ATTITUDE	I'M SATISFIED	NOT SATISFIED
Enthusiasm	———	———
Vision-Dreams	———	———
Tough-Mindedness	———	———
Systematic Planning	———	———
Commitment to Excellence	———	———
Self-Respect and Self-Discipline	———	———
Respect for the Individual	———	———

Figure 16

A cybernetic unit is one in which there is a built-in corrective and improvement system.

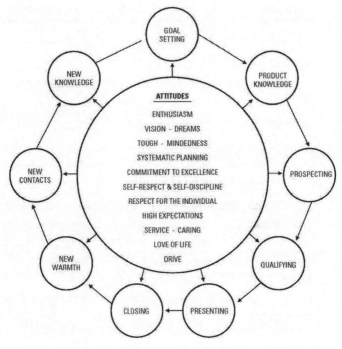

Figure 17

Question: "So what! I made a sale. What is in it for me but a little commission?"

Answer: Through *superior service* we actually confirm and etch out our own identity.

- We make more money, become richer.

- We grow and stretch.

- We feel good inside.

- We build lasting relationships.

- We become more professional.

- We never quit growing.

- Boredom and an ever-improving concept of service and personal growth cannot co-exist.

ATTITUDE	I'M SATISFIED	NOT SATISFIED
Sensitivity-Listening	————	————
High Expectations	————	————
Service-Caring	————	————
Love of Life	————	————
Drive	————	————

Figure 18

Through *affirmation* of the customer's wants, needs, and possibilities, we help them grow in confidence, fulfillment, and satisfaction. That's really what they pay for, as well as the fact that your product, service, and support will enable them to meet or exceed their objectives.

Don't be fooled by superficial indications. Take steps to ensure that they truly feel affirmed, reassured, and motivated by your example.

Remember, who you are and what you represent can resonate so loudly that they'll want to hear what you have to say.

Question: "I've heard that dedication, discipline, and determination are the corner posts of the sales artist. Could you give me a checklist to see how I measure up?"

Answer: The "3 D's" are indeed important cornerstones to any undertaking at the level of art. The following questions provide an ongoing evaluation system to maintain excellence.

Question: "What is the 'Excellent Persuader's' road map for turning dreams into reality?"

Answer: The "Excellent Persuader's" road map is a well-planned sequence of events that is a result of helping the lives of others become richer by developing richness

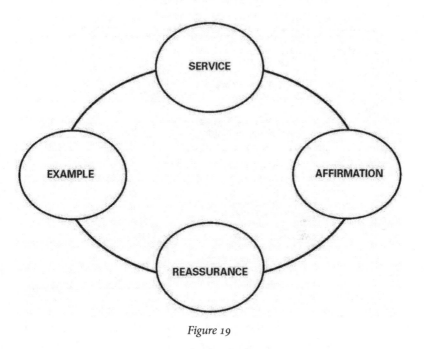

Figure 19

(mental, spiritual, financial, etc . . .) in his/her own life. Study the following illustration and evaluate it in light of your own plan

3 D's	Questions to Ask Yourself	Comments
Dedication	Are you really committed to your profession?	
	Do you believe that your service is the best?	
	Are you convinced that you are helping your customer?	
Discipline	Do you set definite goals and meet them?	
	Do you research the prospect's needs and problems in advance; Anticipate objections?	
	Are you training yourself not to waste either your own or your customer's time?	
Determination	Are you unwilling to settle for a quick "no" answer?	
	When you think that you and the customer are in agreement, do you ask for the order?	
	When you're turned down, do you turn-on?	

Figure 20

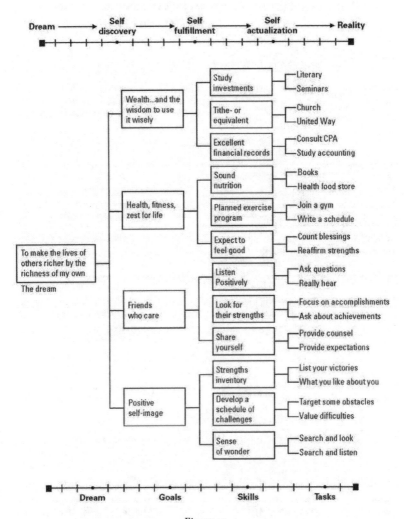

Figure 21

Question: "Some people say the power of a question is infinitely stronger than the power of a statement. Can you share some specific types of questions that can be used?"

	Purposes/Techniques	Example
Open ended Question	1) To elicit response	What do you think about business conditions these days?
	2) Question is vague	
	3) Response of more than a few words is expected	
Direct Question	1) Identifies a restricted topic	What level of profitability are you looking for?
	2) Ask for a restricted reply on a specific topic	What suppliers did you buy from last year?
Closed Question	1) Calls for a specific response in a few words	Do you want this delivered Tuesday? What two methods of shipping do you use?
Mirror Question	1) Non-direct technique	Prospect's statement: "I don't believe in changing suppliers."
	2) Encourages expanding on incomplete answer	Salesperson: "You say you don't believe that changing suppliers can save you money?"
	3) Usually made by restating earlier statement	
Probing Question	1) Asked to elicit more information	"Why is that so?" "Oh, really?"
	2) Can be "why" and "how" questions	
	3) Can use statements like "oh, good," and "I understand," that do not indicate receiver's feelings	
Leading Question	1) Imply or encourage specific answer	"Naturally, you agree with this decision, don't you?"
	2) They lead respondent to an answer the question expects	
	3) Ways of determining if respondent really understands or is genuinely committed	

Figure 22

Question: "What is a 'Strength's Notebook,' and how do I make one?"

Building My Strengths Notebook:

Rationale:

A Strengths Notebook is to help individuals recognize positive characteristics and strengths within themselves. Through the recognition of these strengths, you can entirely shift your current mental and attitudinal paradigms.

Materials:

Pen, notebook or three ring binder with loose leaf paper, three dividers for the notebook.

How to Develop a Strengths Notebook:

A Strengths Notebook is an individual resource and development tool. Begin by dividing the notebook into three sections, leave approximately 15 pages between each section.

1. Section One entitled "My Strengths"

2. Section Two entitled "My Victories"

3. Section Three entitled "How I Overcame my Challenges"

Section 1:

In Section One, give yourself a time limit, and list as many strengths as you can. Once you have done this for three or four sessions, ask trusted advisors to list two or three strengths in your notebook. Many times it will take weeks or months to complete, but set an initial goal of 100 strengths.

Note: This may be perceived as an impossible goal, but it will come easily with time.

Section 2:

In Section Two, give yourself a time limit, and list as many victories as you can. Once you have done this for three or four sessions, ask trusted advisors to list two or three victories in your notebook. Many times it will take weeks or months to complete, but set an initial goal of 100 victories.

Note: These victories do not need to be life altering, sometimes it is simply getting out of bed in the morning, learning how to tie one's shoes as a child, or successfully closing a deal.

Section 3: Section Three provides an excellent opportunity to celebrate victories and remember how you overcame past obstacles. This section may also serve as a journal if you would find that beneficial.

Question: How do I make myself indispensable in the workplace?

Answer: In a time of economic uncertainty, Government bailouts, lay-offs, and job exportation, there has never been a more crucial time to make yourself indispensable to your workplace, team, and organization! In order to accomplish this, you must first ensure you have a job. In addition to following ethical business practices, doing the extra work-completing it exceptionally and promptly, and maintaining punctual work habits, these seven steps below will truly make you indispensable to the workplace.

Seven Steps to Workplace Indispensability

1. Build Positive Relationships (social capital)—Life is a series of opportunities to build positive relationships with others.

2. Build a Support Network—The more positive relationships you surround yourself with, the more likely you are to build a positive reputation, and become indispensable to your environment.

3. Innovate—When you become indispensable to your work environment, freedom for creativity and piloting ideas occurs.

4. Build Trust—When you have the ability to work more freely, implement your ideas, and have more workplace autonomy, confidence is built both within the employee and their supervisor.

5. Be Accountable—Once this confidence has been built, it is the employee's responsibility to enhance the confidence, or dissolve it.

6. Operate With Confidence—To build this confidence, unlock your inner passions for your work, and allow yourself to flourish and grow.

7. Work With Passion—When your true passion is unleashed, your job will not only become enjoyable, but your talents will become recognized by your organization, which leads to promotion and higher earning potential!

Key Words In The
Excellent Persuader's Vocabulary

EXPECT THE BEST	MOTIVATION	GROWTH	MANAGING STRENGTHS	PUT MUSCLE INTO YOUR DREAMS	EXCEED YOURSELF
Gratitude - to self, God, and others	Significance	Personal philosophy	Your strength notebook	Purpose & Direction	Stretch
	Faith	Corporate philosophy	Identifying strengths	Fitness; physical, mental, & spiritual	Self-discipline
Joy	Hope	Openness	Classify strengths		Manage Change
Zest	Love	Vulnerability	Develop strengths	From role to goal	FOR-giveness
Humor	Gratitude	Wonder	Assignment or deployment	Doubt you doubts	Abundance of the spirit
Example	Affirmation	Expectations		Stay un-satisfied	
Candor	Shared Meaning	Warmth	Strength expectations	Action Plans	The Greatest Secret
Care-Share-Dare	Shared Understanding		Measure strengths	Integrity	
Build or destroy	Positive listening		Control Strengths	Timetables	
Objectives	Cybernetics		Counsel - don't advise	Accountability	
Compassion	Evaluate - don't judge		The climate for Strengths	Phonies finish last	

Figure 23

About the Authors

Joe D. Batten M.S. CPAE—The late Mr. Batten was the author of 14 books, over 40 training, management, sales and leadership films and presented to over 3,000 audiences in 17 countries; being the first speaker inducted in the *National Speakers Association* Hall of Fame. His New York Times Best-Selling book, *Tough-Minded Management*, was the first management book to reach #1 in America. Mr. Batten worked directly with over 80% of the Fortune 500 Companies and gave the United States Army the phrase, "Be All You Can Be." Mr. Batten was widely considered the "Sales Training Dean of America." Even Ross Perot calls him his "mentor."

Steve Havemann M.S.—Mr. Havemann brings an expertise in education, training, and development. Through his programmatic work, Mr. Havemann excels at the art of persuasion and business development. Mr. Havemann is a recognized leader within his community and serves on a variety of Boards of Directors. He holds his Masters' Degree in Education from Drake University, with a focus in Training and Development.